ChronoSafe

Tools to Protect Your Investments

Presents

Richard Brown's

REPLICA WATCH REPORT

VOLUME 1

Richard Brown's Replica Watch Report: Volume 1

First Edition

International Standard Book Number: 1-4116-1402-X

Printed in the United States of America

Visit us at: *http://www.replicawatchreport.com*

ChronoSafe Media
14761 Pearl Road #159
Strongsville, OH 44136-5026

admin@chronosafe.com

Prologue

This book is a culmination of nearly a year of planning and work. I'm indebted to several people for their support and encouragement over that time.

I'm grateful to people like Neil Irvine for providing some of the wonderful photographs that are used in this book. He freely gave me access to his library and let me raid it as I saw fit, for this I am indebted. If you like a photograph in this book, it's probably Neil's.

KJM provided many of the comparison shots used throughout the Spotter's Guide section.

I'd also like to thank John Davis and Hannes Braunwarth-Knoebel for their genuine watch photographs. They gave unconditional support to someone who asked for their help out of the blue.

Most of all I'd like to thank my beautiful wife who put up with my late night sessions in front of the computer and my mumbling about picture resizing and Rolex case numbers. She has always been my rock.

I hope you enjoy this project. It will be updated officially often to reflect new information and correct any errors in the existing text. This is a living document, always growing and changing.

You can find up-to-the-minute revisions and updates on the web site: *www.replicawatchreport.com*, where I'll also post the up coming changes to the next edition. I want this guide to be a reflection on the ever-changing replica market.

— *Richard Brown*

Table of Contents

Caveat

It's important to realize that even in the world of genuine watches there is variance and change between model years and even individual watches. So what could be inaccurate on one watch could be totally correct on another. Aftermarket parts and non-authorized repairs also can account for inaccuracies in individual watches from a factory's standard.

Therefore, this book is meant as a reference and a guide; it's NOT to be taken as the final word. Don't make decisions solely based on the information presented in this book; use the resources you have around you, including authorized dealers, the Internet, and the manufacturers themselves.

The only true way to determine a watch's authenticity is to send the watch back to the manufacturer for evaluation. Not even they can make an accurate appraisal based on photographs or video images.

There is no substitution for buying a watch at a reputable authorized dealer. If you want 100% assurance of a watch's origins, buy new from such a reseller. All other sources have a certain level of risk associated with them.

The Replicas Used in this Book

The replicas in this book are for reference purposes only. I don't condone the practice of buying, selling, or trading counterfeit watches. Please don't contact me for pricing or purchase information on the replica watches photographed in this book. Please don't ask me where to find replica dealers online, or ask which dealer has the most accurate product. Remember that replicas are illegal and detract from the genuine brand's profit and identity. We all end up paying for this with higher prices and lower resale values of our watches in the future.

Introduction

A long time watch collector, I've seen an alarming trend growing in the hobby. Counterfeiters of high quality watches have been flooding the market with look-a-likes that are becoming more and more difficult to quickly separate from the genuine article. This has alarmed me, mainly because of the general lack of knowledge of replicas by the general watch buyer.

The purpose for this book is to aid the collector and buyer in determining the level of risk that a watch is counterfeit, especially when buying from an auction house like eBay where you are relying on the honesty of the seller when making a purchase.

At one time the quality of counterfeit watches was so poor it was fairly obvious to the layman when they came across one at a flea market or went shopping online. The poor materials and shoddy build quality spoke volumes when it came to scrutinizing the watch. They looked "fake" and had a costume jewelry feel to them. No more.

Today's counterfeits have benefited tremendously from a number of factors: the introduction of CNC equipment to the Far East, the advent of the Internet as a sales and distribution channel, and most of all, the availability of higher quality parts such as ETA movements and cheap sapphire crystals that has helped fuel the revolution of small independent watch manufacturers today.

These factors have contributed to raising the bar in the quality of the average counterfeit watch. A new breed of high-end replicas allows the manufacturers to invest more in each model.

The Internet has introduced a new upscale market that is willing to pay up to $1,500 for a replica Rolex President. That allows both a tremendous profit for the manufacturer and reseller, and allows them the money to make more accurate watches in the future.

I've watched this market grow at an alarming rate over the last two years, from a few low key sellers advertising on mailing lists and message boards, to the now growing list of online web sites catering to those that want replica Rolex watches, the trend towards a higher quality counterfeit continues to find a place in cyber space. Purchasers who buy these watches for their own amusement and curiosity are not the long-term problem in my opinion. The real danger comes from those looking to defraud other people by misrepresenting replicas as genuine.

One look at eBay watch sales provides a good example of where the danger lies. Search for "Rolex" and look carefully at some of the listings. At any given time there are over 5,000 entries for Rolex watches and accessories. Of this number probably 20% are listings for counterfeit goods, or worse, pictures of real watches that will result in the delivery of a replica. Because of the rampant illegal activity on eBay many auctions for Rolex watches close with no bids. People are incredibly wary of sellers, and rightfully scrutinize each transaction.

> **"*Don't be fooled by your impressions of counterfeit watches from even a short time ago...*"**

This book could save you thousands of dollars by giving you the tools to recognize the signs that may indicate a watch is a counterfeit. We'll show you what warning signs to look for in auction listings, as well as provide detailed information on individual watch models. This book is a quick reference guide designed to be taken with you when shopping at flea markets or pawn shops to give you quick tips on what to look for when examining a watch.

This book isn't an exhaustive research tool on replicas. We never open watch to check the movement, for example. The examinations recommended here are noninvasive. They're meant to be done quickly, with the purpose of assigning risk, not authenticity.

I see this guide being useful also to those professionals at jewelry stores or auction houses that need help in quickly assessing the possibility that a watch is counterfeit. Unethical people may try swap a replica watch in for a genuine watch during a routine browsing session. When dealing with high-end watches this kind of fraud could result in the loss of thousands of dollars to the dealer.

Don't be fooled by your impressions of counterfeit watches from even just a short time ago. Just as every other industry has taken advantage of new technology, so have the counterfeiters. While not up to the quality of the genuine brands they imitate, they can provide a very close perception of the real thing.

Anatomy of a Watch

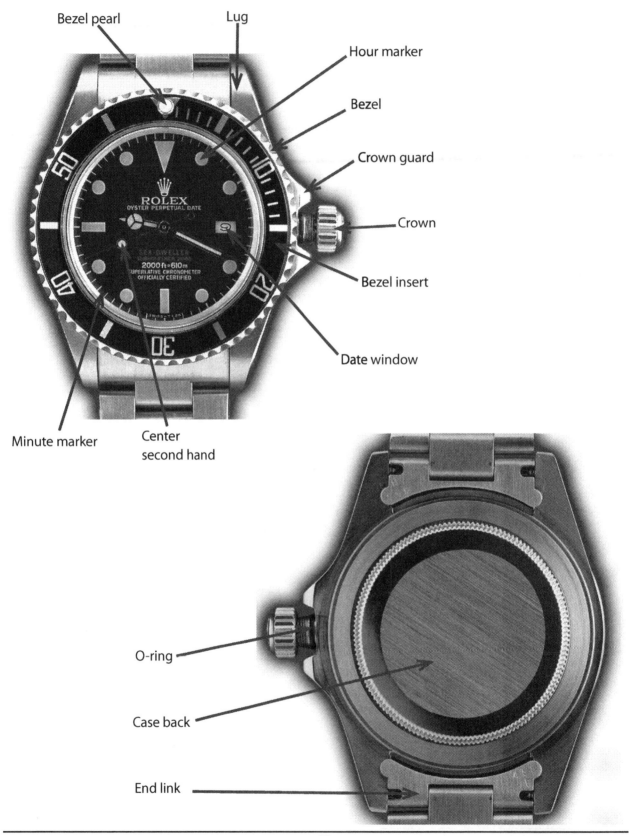

Bezel pearl

Lug

Hour marker

Bezel

Crown guard

Crown

Bezel insert

Date window

Minute marker

Center second hand

O-ring

Case back

End link

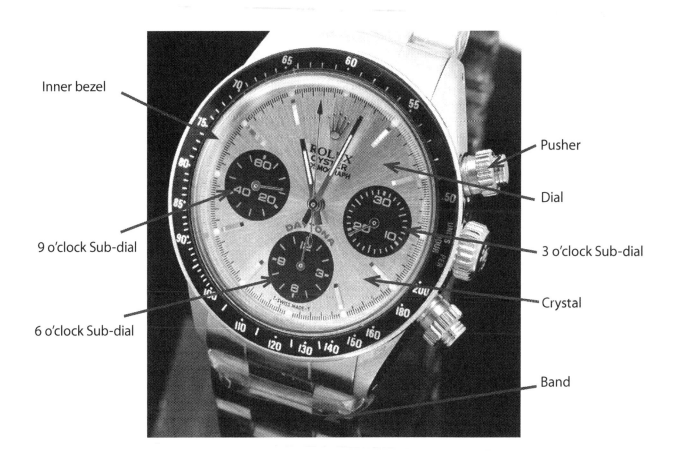

Inner bezel

Pusher

Dial

9 o'clock Sub-dial

3 o'clock Sub-dial

Crystal

6 o'clock Sub-dial

Band

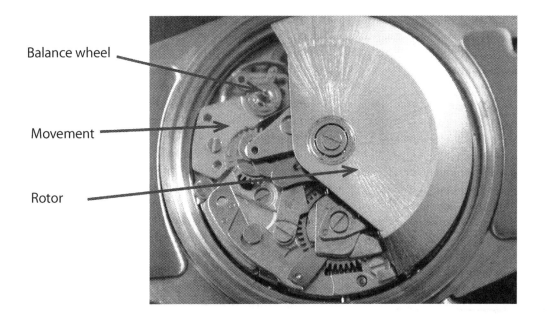

Balance wheel

Movement

Rotor

The Making of a Replica

Most replica watches claim to be "Swiss made," attempting to gain an aura of authenticity and quality. In reality, most replica watches are actually made in Asia: China, Thailand, or Taiwan. This is because the labor rates there are greatly reduced, and the factories that produce them are producing legitimate replacement parts or watches of other marks. Also, law enforcement is not as diligent about protecting copyrights as they are in the West.

Replica watch movements are typically of Japanese or Chinese manufacture, although the high-end watches may have actual Swiss-made movements. ETA (*www.eta.ch*) movements are a popular substitute for many Rolex and other high-end replicas. The movement is made in Switzerland, although Asian factories are now producing copies of the movements in their own factories. One reason for this is that ETA is limiting the sale of OEM movements which threatens the availability for replica manufacturers.

A number of factories are simply two- or three-man assembly shops taking parts from bins and assembling the watches by hand. There is no quality control, and two watches from the same factory can differ in fit and finish quite easily. With the bulk of the replica watches being inexpensive models that sell for under $50 there is no great need for precision assembly.

While most parts for replica watches are produced in Asia, the assembly of watches can occur anywhere in the world. Germany, Italy, and the United States are locations where there is a thriving businesses in assembling replicas. They can legitimately order the various OEM parts (movements, cases, bands) as replacements for damaged parts for branded watches. Then the various parts can be assembled with a counterfeit dial to create a replica of a particular original model.

Some sellers actually use "homage" brand watches such as Geneva and RWX and replace the dials with famous branded dials producing easy to make (and real feeling) replicas.

To be sold in the United States they must be shipped into the country. A portion of replicas arriving through customs are confiscated or assessed as real and a custom duty applied to them. But through a variety of methods a large number of watches make it into the country on a daily basis.

The ETA Movement

Most high-end replicas use the ubiquitous ETA brand of movements. They are used because they are relatively inexpensive (Ofrei, an aftermarket vendor, lists ETA movements for as little as $40 in quantity) and have been proven to be highly reliable and provide a good imitation of branded watch movements. This is because ETA provides the movements for many of the current watch manufacturers in OEM form. These movements may later be tweaked or modified, but in reality they perform almost identically to their base model's statistics.

Breitling is a good example of a manufacturer that relies on ETA for movements. Several of Breitling's models use a modified ETA movement in their design. This movement is tuned by replacing some parts with higher performance pieces, or improving the finish and tolerances of the movement. Still, at the heart of the watch beats a simple ETA movement.

There are several ETA models used extensively in the production of Rolex replicas:

Movement	Model
ETA 2893-A2	GMT Master II, Explorer II
ETA 2834-2	Day Date
ETA 2836-2	Submariner, DateJust, Sea-Dweller
Valjoux 7750	Daytona

These movements are easy to use and accept aftermarket Rolex-style hands and cases. These movements also have the smooth sweep and hacking features available with modern Rolex watches. As a note, Rolex currently uses in-house movements for their watches. This will eventually lead to Rolex offering features and styles that are more difficult for the aftermarket to emulate. An example of this is the post-2000 Rolex Daytona model that uses a new Rolex chronograph movement. With its second hand at the 6 o'clock sub-dial, this movement has yet to be emulated by any replica on the market.

Clones of the Clone

ETA is going to begin restricting the OEM market for their movements. This will reduce the flow of ETA movements being used in replicas and legitimate watches alike. In preparation for this change, Asian manufacturers are beginning to produce copies of the ETA movements. These copies are functionally identical to the ETA models, though they are typically made of lower quality materials or with looser tolerances than ETA will allow. This is having an effect of lowering the cost to produce replicas while ensuring a source for movements without relying on a specific manufacturer.

Other Movements

New to the replica scene is the use of other OEM movements to emulate genuine watches. Lemania 861, Poljot 3133, and the Unitas 6497 are all movements used to emulate current famous brand production watches. The Lemania is a base for the movement used in several Omega watches. The Poljot is used frequently to emulate vintage Daytonas and Patek Philippe chronographs (the Poljot has two functional sub-dials). The Unitas is an OEM version of the movement used in base model Panerais. Newer examples of this movement are even decorated with Panerai engraving to make them more convincing.

The Manufacturing Process

The manufacturing process has been made easier through the use of computers. Most manufacturers have CNC machines that can carve cases and other watch parts from solid pieces of steel. Remember that a great number of the larger of these factories don't solely produce replicas; their main business may be producing replacement parts or other legitimate branded watches.

The replica manufacturer typically buys in bulk the various parts they need to complete a watch. For example, they will buy hands from one OEM seller and dials from another. These relationships mean that no one manufacturer is soley responsible for the creation of any one given replica. It also means since parts are purchased in quantity that minor modifications of replicas are rare until the existing stock is used up. An example of this are the enameled blue hands used in many replicas today.

One of the biggest problems that replica manufacturers face is the language barrier. While most watches have dials and markings printed in English, most of the people designing the replicas don't speak the language! This leads to a number of errors that creep into the replica design; the makers are simply copying letter by letter, never really understanding what they're spelling.

Distribution

The Internet has provided a huge distribution channel for the replica manufacturer. Instead of selling product to street vendors and mail order shops they have been able to branch into selling watches to a variety of reseller web sites scattered throughout the cyber space.

The Internet retailers offer a variety of price points for their products, which typically have nothing to do with the cost of the actual watch from the manufacturer. Many misrepresent the quality of the replicas in an effort to dupe buyers into spending hundreds, if not thousands of dollars on a product they spent very little to acquire. Replicas can cost as little as $5 to produce.

These web sites tout the quality of these watches and use marketing terms such as "triple wrapped gold" and "improved 2004 model" in order to make it appear there is inherent value in spending $700 to $1,500 on a replica. Little do these buyers know that they're chasing a pipe dream.

The cold reality is that there is little if no difference between the ETA-based replicas sold by these vendors. While some may use pictures of real Rolexes to represent their product the reality is these watches are simply stainless steel and gold plated copies that hardly come close to the genuine watch in quality.

These resellers typically operate just a step ahead of the law. Their sites come and go with regularity and they are careful to leave as little trace of themselves as they can. Very few of them, for example, offer a telephone number as a means of contact. Rolex has been stepping up their effort in eliminating these predatory dealers from the Internet.

The High End

Most replica watches are mass-produced for the tourist trade. They are of a low quality and can typically be spotted as counterfeit with some knowledge of what to look for. Still, there is a small subset of replica manufacturers that are making higher quality watches that adapt with the changes in the market more quickly than their counterparts. These are the real reason why this book was written.

These higher-end manufacturers have been responsive in providing changes to their product to meet the needs of a small but vocal subset of replica buyers. These people are knowledgeable of the flaws in typical replicas and are looking for and willing to pay higher prices for watches that correct these problems. The result is watches that have improved year to year in their quality and appearance.

These watches cost more to produce and therefore there is more risk in the distribution; losing a watch to customs incurs a greater loss. Remember that there is inherent risk in shipping counterfeit goods around the world. The prices charged for these watches tend to reflect these risks.

Many of these higher-end watches are based on the ETA brand of movements. They copy a range of manufacturers from Audemars Piguet to Rolex. Unlike the traditional replica manufacturers whose higher-end watches are strictly Rolex, these manufacturers can produce watches from brands like Panerai and Omega.

It's important to realize that these watches represent a small subset of the output from the replica factories. But this level of quality makes them some of the most dangerous replicas produced. We'll be showing you some of these watches in the Spotter's Guide section.

Frankenwatches

Another type of watch that can be difficult (if not impossible in some cases) to identify are "Frankenwatches". This term comes from the practice of assembling a watch from a variety of genuine and or replica parts that produce a watch that appears to be made by a particular brand but in reality has no warranty and no identity with the legal manufacturer.

An example of this is the common practice of buying Rolex watch cases and crystals from eBay. One can source the remaining parts from a variety of legitimate dealers online such as Ofrei who sells aftermarket replacement parts for Rolex watches. Purchasing a DateJust case and buying an aftermarket band, ETA movement, dial, and hands produces a watch that has a legitimate serial number (from the case) but is in reality simply a collection of parts.

Some unscrupulous people will even take a genuine stainless steel Rolex apart and remove the movement and dial and put them in an aftermarket solid gold case. This provides an immediate rise in the apparent value from the original stainless steel watch. This practice is one of the reasons why there are so many empty stainless steel cases for sale on eBay at any one time. This is a popular substitution is Japan and Hong Kong. There are recently several known examples of solid gold 18 karat Rolex Presidents on the replica market; some using genuine Rolex movements and dials.

The trouble with these watches from an identification standpoint is they can be made completely from genuine parts. Some people purchase rare dials (such as double red Sea-Dweller or single red Submariner) and retrofit them on a less valuable watch of the same model. This process results in a watch that may only be differentiated from a legitimate example of that rare model by its serial number, or by sending the watch back to the original manufacturer for identification.

The best weapon against the Frankenwatches is to be very diligent in your research during the buying process. Know what your watch should have in terms of features and markings. Also, it's important always to "buy the seller"; in other words, have confidence in the seller's reputation and honesty. It's critical to check the seller's references, and whenever possible handle the transaction in person and inspect the watch with the seller present before purchasing.

If you personally don't have the expertise to evaluate a watch, spend the extra money and enlist the aid of a known expert in that particular model. Still, the only definite way to determine the authenticity of the watch is to have it sent back to the manufacturer or perhaps to a very knowledgeable factory dealer.

Know Your Watch

Before you go and spend your hard-earned money on an online purchase, I strongly recommend you do your homework. The web has many excellent resources for those looking to learn about their favorite watch or watch brand. Go into any purchase armed with this information and you've won half the battle of avoiding expensive missteps.

While doing your research, gather as much information as you can. Get the dimensions of the watch. Examine closely the dial features and case back (download photos if you can). Your best tools here are your eyes and hands. Whenever possible, visit a local dealer of the watch brand and handle the watch in person. This will give you an idea of the weight and appearance of the watch when you go shopping.

There are several places on the Internet to aid you in your research. Here are a couple of my favorites:

Timezone – *http://www.timezone.com*

One of my favorite watch web sites is Timezone. It's full of very knowledgeable people who are quite willing to help you by providing information or answering questions. Their forums on individual watch brands makes for valuable reading. Also, the "Sales Corner" has some excellent deals from very reliable (in my experience) sellers.

The PuristS – *http://www.thepurists.com*

This web site is a bit more analytical than Timezone, but filled with great watch reviews and an awesome library of pictures and articles. If you're a fan of high-end watches, nearly every major brand is covered. One of the best research sites on the web.

Watchuseek – *http://www.watchuseek.com*

This is an excellent site to gather pricing information and photos on the watches you're interested in. It's also a great online resource for purchasing watches themselves. Probably one of the better organized watch sites on the web.

WatchNet – *http://www.watchnet.com*

WatchNet's claim to fame is their Trading Post. Both dealers and individuals list new and used watches for sale. This is an excellent place to shop and gather valuable information about your favorite watch model. Be aware that dealers as well as individuals sell their watches here.

Paneristi – *http://www.paneristi.com*

The best site online for information on Panerai watches. If you're looking for reference information, or to purchase from their thriving online community, it's a valuable resource of all things Panerai. Their guide to deciphering Panerai model numbers is invaluable.

Atlantic Time – *http://www.atlantictime.com*

Atlantic Time is a commercial dealer on the web that stocks excellent images of their catalog online. This allows you to research models and pricing (they list retail and their discounted price on the site) all in one place. It's one of my first stops when researching a model I'm not familiar with. I've never purchased a watch from them, but they seem to be a long standing vendor and I haven't seen any complaints about their service. Unfortunately, they are no longer a Rolex reseller.

Forum Etiquette

When using these forums, always be aware that there are rules and regulations associated with each one. Always read carefully the posting instructions to avoid breaking these rules. Read the categories and make sure you post your inquiry in the proper section. You'll get the best results to questions when you respect the culture of the board from whom you're asking for help.

First, read old messages posted on the board. There's a good chance that someone else has asked your question earlier and has gotten a response. By reading the previous posts you may get your answer immediately and you'll avoid annoying people by asking the same question. If you don't see the answer to your question then make a post asking clearly and concisely; preferably with questions that can be answered with a yes or no.

Next, be patient! If someone doesn't respond immediately it doesn't mean you're being ignored. Realize that many of these boards have members that live all around the world. People may not be online when you post your question. Give it a day before you follow up your initial question with another request for a response. Remember, this help is free; no one is obligated to reply. Always thank people that do post an answer.

Search Engines

Another excellent source to use when doing research are search engines. Google is the Oracle at Delphi for our generation. By using specific search criteria you can find information on nearly every brand made; both objective information from reviews of watch models to subjective opinions on forums. To restrict the search from listing replica watches, use "-replica" at the end of your search criteria. For example, if you were interested in finding out about Panerais you could type "Panerai -replica" to get a listing of pages that were about Panerai, but didn't include any replica sites.

Watch Manufacturer's Web Sites and Catalogs

Never underestimate the value of the manufacturer's own web site when doing research. Some are just marketing vehicles and have very little real information (Rolex's site is guilty of this). Other sites, such as Breitling's, have a wealth of information and pictures that can be used to comparison shop or to review before buying online.

These sites can also give you valuable insight into the construction of their watches. This includes detailed photos and multimedia presentations. Breiting and Tag Heuer have some excellent articles and presentations on the quality of their manufacturing process. Absorb this information before you go shopping.

Grab a list of the local retailers for the brand. Most manufacturers will list their major dealers on their web site. Visit the dealers in your area and use the opportunity to see and handle the genuine watch. Sometimes the dealers will also carry customer watches for sale on consignment. You get an opportunity to buy a slightly used watch that has a known pedigree. Always inquire and find out!

They also have catalogs of the brands they carry that they will give you just for inquiring. These catalogs are wonderful reference tools; they include photographs and statistics on each of the models a brand produces. Some people are selling these catalogs on eBay, but in reality they're there for the asking, for free. If your local dealer is out of catalogs request one from the manufacturer by mail.

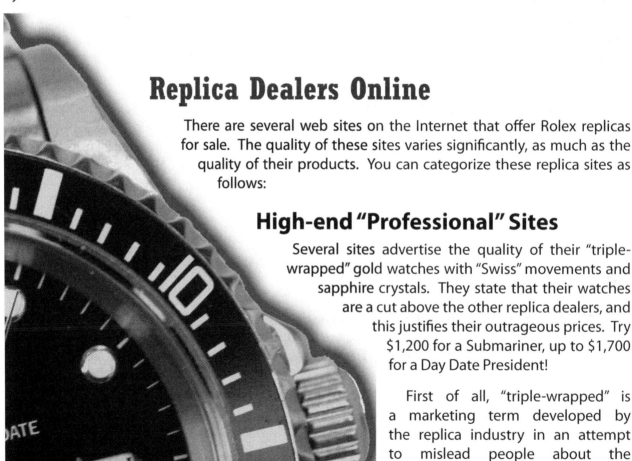

Replica Dealers Online

There are several web sites on the Internet that offer Rolex replicas for sale. The quality of these sites varies significantly, as much as the quality of their products. You can categorize these replica sites as follows:

High-end "Professional" Sites

Several sites advertise the quality of their "triple-wrapped" gold watches with "Swiss" movements and sapphire crystals. They state that their watches are a cut above the other replica dealers, and this justifies their outrageous prices. Try $1,200 for a Submariner, up to $1,700 for a Day Date President!

First of all, "triple-wrapped" is a marketing term developed by the replica industry in an attempt to mislead people about the manufacturing process. They claim it's a process that layers different grades of gold on the case and band that results in a thick durable quality finish that's solid gold throughout. In reality these watches follow the same gold plating that most of the other replicas use.

"Swiss" is a term used to indicate the use of ETA movements in the watch design. ETA movements have tended to be more reliable in the past than Asian movements, which tend to be made from a cheaper metal with less quality control. In reality these same Asian movement makers are now producing clones of the ETA movements themselves! These dealers charge a premium for these watches over the "Non-Swiss" models.

"Japanese" Sites

Selling admittedly lesser-quality watches, these sites try to lure you into a $150-$250 purchase of a counterfeit Rolex, or other brand. These watches, to put it mildly, are typically of poor quality. With their incorrect date fonts and horrible crystals and bands, any reader of this book could spot one easily even from a photograph. These watches use Miyota movements (which actually can be excellent movements in genuine watches such as Seiko) or cheaper Asian movements that have a noticeable "tick" in the motion which again makes them easier to spot.

The Other Guys

Finally, there are a number of smaller sites that sell cheap tourist counterfeits that you could buy for $20 on New York's Canal Street if you were so inclined. Unfortunately these sites would try to gouge you for $100.

None of the sites are reliable, listed with the Better Business Bureau, or even bother to post a phone number to allow you to contact them. Remember this is an illegal business and they stay one step ahead of the law, and therefore could disappear at a moment's notice.

Other Brands

While Rolex is the most popular watch brand to copy, there are several other brands that are developing a following in the replica market. Cartier, Omega, Panerai, Patek Philippe, and Vacheron Constantin are all falling victim to more and more accurate replicas. Just because the watch you are interested in is not a Rolex does not make it a safe purchase.

Buying Replicas

I know some people will buy this guide as reference tool for purchasing replicas. While I don't condone this I can't ignore the fact that it will happen. For those people I want to provide assistance on how to avoid misinformation.

There are several "review" web sites that claim to collect and categorize data about the products various online replica vendors provide. They are in truth house organs for the "recommended" sites and are used to bash their competition and convince buyers they are buying quality merchandise.

It's been my experience that these sites are dangerous simply because they mix enough facts with their fiction to make their misinformation seem plausible. They offer articles describing the difference between replica watches, yet use these articles to justify the high prices and sales tactics being used by their own sites.

They recommend COD over credit card payments, saying they are less risky and provide safety. The actual truth is the opposite; with a credit card purchase you would have protection from a vendor by being able to contest the transaction. COD is a form of cash; you are normally not allowed to inspect the package before you pay for it. The carrier has no liability for your transaction. By paying with COD you lose your easiest options to pursue the seller if something goes wrong.

The Value of Replicas

Replica watches are sold on the Internet for a variety of prices. You can find dealers online that have slick commercial sites and people who sell from photo galleries and e-mail accounts. The main thing to remember is that all of these goods are counterfeit and don't meet the level of standards set by the original product.

The fancier replica sites try to entice you by declaring that their product is of a higher quality. They talk about "triple-wrapped gold" and "Swiss manufacturing"; in reality, they sell the same quality product that nearly every other vendor on the Internet has access to. There isn't any special process or different manufacturing steps that make these watches different. It's all about presentation.

So, those Gold Rolex Day-Date Presidents they price at $1,200 are probably purchased from a vendor in Hong Kong for $50. The Submariner they have list for $700 they probably bought for $40. The only value they have is in the perception that the buyer has developed. These sites make their money by hyping up their product, and preying on unsuspecting and naive customers.

There is almost no inherent quality in a replica watch. Sure, it may look like a Rolex or a Patek Philippe, but in reality it's simply a cheap, mass-produced watch with no resale value at all. Remember, there is no secondary market for replicas. With a genuine watch, you can always resell it on web sites like Timezone or Watchuseek. There is no legitimate option for reselling a replica watch. Once you buy it, the watch is yours unless you want to tempt fate and prosecution trying to represent it as genuine.

While Rolex spends on average a year in manufacturing one of their watches, most replica shops can put together a counterfeit Rolex in a day. They simply grab a movement right from a pile of OEM parts and slap a watch together. While legitimate manufacturers will tune and lubricate their movements before using them, the counterfeiters will use a movement "dry," without any preparation or quality testing. This means that movement won't have the same lifespan that a movement in a genuine watch will have.

Servicing replicas is another issue; most watch repair shops won't work on a counterfeit watch. If you have any issues with the watch you're really on your own. Don't count on any "warranty" that the dealer may claim to offer. You'll be lucky to get reach them again once they have your money. If you sank $1,200 in a replica Rolex and it doesn't work one day, you might have just learned a valuable (albeit expensive) lesson. Had that watch been a genuine Omega or Breitling, your watch would be covered by a warranty and a dedicated service organization.

Read everything on the Internet with a grain of salt. While there are usually some kernels of truth on these sites about replicas, at the end of the day they are looking to sell you a bill of goods. None of the online replica web sites have your best interest at heart. There are no warranties, return policies, or customer service departments. While they may claim otherwise, once they get your money they'll have little or nothing to do with you.

Genuine Manufacturer's Take on Counterfeiting

Rolex, Cartier, and the other genuine manufacturers take the protection of their products very seriously. At one point, when the quality of the replicas was so low, Rolex didn't take an active role in seeking out and eliminating replica dealers. It was a well known fact that a visit to New York's Canal Street could net you several Rolex replicas just by looking around and inquiring. Several dealers were selling replicas down the street from legitimate Rolex resellers.

Today, Rolex and the other makers are aggressively seeking out and prosecuting dealers and resellers. American law enforcement, including U.S. Customs, is getting involved in the process; it's a felony to copy and resell protected works. Because of this, some replica resellers are becoming more elusive in their dealings, insisting on "cash" in the form of money orders, cashier's checks, or COD.

Cash allows the dealers to hide their transactions. There's no credit card record of purchases or deposits. Without these records it's more difficult to prove sales volume, and in turn the monetary liability they may have. THIS is the true reason certain sites recommend COD transactions.

Rolex is now implementing a variety of anti-countefeiting methods in their newest watches. These include a tiny engraved crown on the crystal of many models, as well as the name "ROLEX" printed under the crystal on the sides of the dial, sometimes called the inner-bezel. Both of these methods have already been duplicated (with varying success) by the replica makers. To date, Rolex's most successful change has been in the use of the new post-2000 movement in the Daytona. This movement has no comparable ETA or Japanese clone, and therefore it's difficult to duplicate. To date no replica manufacturer has correctly copied the new Daytona

Remember, a replica is a copy of the original made as cheaply as possible. It only has the look, but not the quality, of the original. Caveat Emptor!

Spotter's Tips

There are a variety of common flaws and mistakes that permeate the counterfeit market. This chapter will look at these in detail, and will show you things to review when you need to quickly evaluate a watch. Even the replica watches not included in the Spotter's Guide later in this book will probably exhibit some of these flaws, enabling you to categorize risk when deciding on a purchase.

While the focus of this book is on Internet purchasing, all of the information provided here should be helpful when buying watches at flea markets or estate sales. Use this book as a study guide to prepare you for what to look for when you're interested in purchasing.

Picture Quality

First, we have to establish a level of acceptable picture quality when attempting to evaluate a watch. Some people post tiny grainy pictures, with little light, and try to sell watches worth thousands of dollars. Honestly, how someone thinks people will be willing to part with their hard earned cash from some postage stamp-sized fuzzy image is beyond me.

My advice on all of these sales is to pass them by, no matter how good the reputation of the seller or how good the price. The odds are not with you when you can't evaluate the watch before the purchase. Either ask the owner for better pictures or just assume the watch isn't worth the money. Read the chapter on eBay buys for more information.

Look for auctions with large pictures taken from several angles. This will allow you to validate several aspects of a watch you may have missed from a single picture.

The Tools

Everyone interested in buying or collecting high-end watches should invest in some simple tools. All of these can be purchased over the web from sources like eBay for a total investment of less than $50. These can be used when you have an opportunity to inspect a watch in person.

Jeweler's loupe – A jeweler's loupe is a great way to inspect various parts of a watch up close. 2.5x magnification loupes are the least expensive, but I would recommend spending a bit more and get the 10x loupe. These loupes can be found typically for around $5 to $20 dollars, and are probably the most valuable tool you can buy.

A loupe is a magnifying glass designed for inspecting details up close. They are used by jewelers and photographers to look for flaws and imperfections that the eye by itself can't spot.

Spring bar tool – If you're interested in verifying the serial number on a Rolex, the spring bar tool can help you (or the person selling the watch if they require) carefully remove the band. You need to do this to reveal the serial and model numbers between the lugs. A spring bar tool is typically $10.

Ruler – A cheap plastic metric ruler can be used to verify sizes of cases and strap widths. Also, the thickness of many replicas is greater than their genuine counterparts (Patek Philippe is an example of where this is common), so knowing what the thickness should be will greatly aid in evaluating suspect watches.

Pocket flashlight – Want to test the luminosity of a watch? Shine a flashlight directly onto the surface for a few seconds and cup your hands around it to see the results. Some replicas have flawed dials or bezels that don't glow brightly enough (or at all) in comparison to the original. Don't rely on sunlight or the room lights to give you an accurate accounting of the luminosity.

An even better option are the small locket LED key chain lights that are being sold today. These tiny lights fit in your pocket yet produce a very bright and intense light; more intense than any bulb flashlight its size can produce. I've found by holding one of these lights to a crystal of a watch I can instantly charge the dial's luminosity and watch the decay as I turn the light source off. It's a small yet handy device to use during your inspection.

Polishing cloth – A decent jewelry polishing cloth can be used to remove fingerprints and other contaminants and allow you to look at the actual surface of the watch. You can use this to look for scratches, cracks, and other flaws that may have been masked by dirt or smudges.

This book! – Bring this book as a reference along with you as you're browsing. It's easy to forget simple things to look for if you rely on your memory.

Place all these tools in a small bag or carry them in your briefcase. You'll be glad you had them along at some point during your shopping trip.

The First Glance

When you're evaluating a watch, either in person or via photograph, the first thing you should do is step back and view the watch from a mental distance. Look at the "appearance" of the watch. Does it look like it's of a good build quality? Does the crystal have scratches or appear to be dull (possible indication of glass)? Does the crown look screwed in evenly into the case? Examine the band, does it look cheap or feel

light? Are there pins in the band holding the links together on a Rolex for example? Brand new Rolexes have a brilliant, "gem-like" appearance.

You can eliminate many of the lower end counterfeits simply by looking at the watch with an eye that expects to see quality. Rolexes, for example, are made exceedingly well and don't have sloppy dial printing or glued-on parts. Don't expect a Patek Philippe to look cheap; use your common sense. If the watch doesn't look like quality then it probably isn't. The one exception to make here is to give some lee-way to vintage models. 25 year-old Submariners will have a bit more variance than a new one.

If you have the opportunity to hold the watch (This is something which I recommend strongly. Never make a purchase in person without being able to closely examine the merchandise) feel the weight of the watch. A real stainless steel Rolex weighs on average about 140 grams. The band should feel substantial and not "tinny" or lightweight. Look at the watch objectively as if you were purchasing it for your boss, with his money…

Whenever possible try to examine any paperwork and receipts. The paperwork should match the serial number engraved on the watch. If it doesn't match then be very wary. Receipts are good to have; it proves when the watch was purchased, as well as where. This becomes important whenever you need to prove the watch's pedigree in the future. Always ask for all accessories (boxes, hang tags) and paperwork (warranty, receipt, owner's manuals) whenever buying a watch, new or used. You never know what a future owner might be interested in (I had a buyer get excited because I had the plastic bezel protector that ships with the watch).

Top Ten Replica Flaws

So you found the watch of your dreams. The seller doesn't want an arm and a leg for it either! What can you do to quickly check for counterfeiting? We're not talking an in-depth review, just a few things that are obvious "tells" that will alert us we're looking at a replica watch. I've categorized ten things that are always dead give-aways whenever I look at a watch or a photograph. Review these and apply these tests to a watch your examining:

1. The Crystal: Look for Reflections

Some manufacturers such as Panerai, Zenith, Corum, Girard Perregaux and Breitling (unfortunately not Rolex) use a thin coating on the surface of the crystal to reduce the effects of reflections. This tends to give the crystal a slight blue tint but can render it near transparent at most viewing angles. If the watch you're inspecting is any one of these brands and not a vintage model, be concerned if there are a large number of reflections from the crystal at varying angles.

> *Rolex watches don't have exhibition backs.*

Modern high-end watches use an artificial sapphire for the crystal, as opposed to the treated glass that many low-end replicas use. The surest way to test for sapphire is to take the watch to a reliable watch repair shop. Sapphire is nearly as hard as a diamond and a true sapphire crystal would be resistant to scratching. Some people rely on misting water on the surface to look for beading, but I consider this an unreliable method. Typically sapphire is very transparent with sharp refractions while glass tends towards a greenish tint at the edges with undefined refraction.

2. The Case: Exhibition or Display Back

Where most replicas fall short is when the original watch has a see-through case back allowing the viewing of the movement. These watches tend to be hand-wound or automatic and have decorative effects such as polished gears and a Côtes de Geneve (wave-like patterns) finish on the movement. Most genuine manufacturers make their watch stand out with a truly beautiful presentation from this exhibition back.

Counterfeit watches, which rely on inexpensive unfinished Swiss or Asian movements, which have no decorations, are at a distinct disadvantage here. These watches reveal a very plain movement with little or no detail. The pieces of the movement look like they have been stamped from sheet metal (which is pretty much the case. These movements are highly mass-produced). One glance at the exposed movement will reveal the watch as counterfeit. Even attempts to dress up the plain movement with gold-tone plating and engraving fall short of the original.

The one notable exception to the rule with exhibition backs are the new replicas coming onto the market that use movements similar to the original watches. The Omega Speedmaster Professional, for example, uses a modified version of a Lemania 861 movement which looks beautiful behind an exhibition back. Several counterfeit watch makers are using this base movement to replicate the look of the original Omega with good success. Panerai, with their use of the Unitas 6497, is also vulnerable to copycats using the original base movement.

3. The Crown: One Piece or Fake

Cheap replicas (typically Rolex copies) might have the logo actually glued to the end of the crown. These watches have so many other flaws that this won't be your first indication of problems. Make sure the crown shows no sign of glue or uneven edges. Also, the watch should wind smooth and free, without the feel of the movement moving in the case.

Some replicas emulate the engraving at the end of a crown with laser etching. Laser etching has no depth to it (if you run your fingernail over the surface it doesn't "catch" in the grooves of the letters like it would for true engraving) and is rarely used on genuine watches. Laser etching has a "frosted" appearance.

Finally, some watches have jewels embedded in the end of the crown (Cartier comes to mind). On genuine watches this jewel is usually a precious or semi-precious stone like a sapphire or ruby. This stone will "sparkle" and have depth to the surface when examined. Replicas typically use a glass or crystal stone to copy the real thing. It normally can be picked out by its dull color or "glassy" appearance.

4. The Band: Cheap and Tinny?

Watches come with either leather/rubber/carbon fiber straps or metal bands. Straps are easy to replace and customize to the owner's taste. That means a cheap department store strap takes 2 minutes to put on a genuine Patek Philippe if the owner wants it that way. When it comes to bands, ask if it's original and look at the lining. Quality watch bands are padded or have a soft leather inner section. Just because it's stamped with the manufacturer's name does not mean it's original.

Metal bands, on the other hand, are harder to duplicate. Most counterfeit watches with metal bands fall into two categories: cheap and tinny, or fairly close. A few of them, though, have nearly the same quality of build that the genuine watch has.

The cheaper bands are made of low-grade stainless steel or are even made of inexpensive pressed sheeting. They typically are held together with pins instead of the screws that most genuine manufacturers use (note that Omega does use pins in their bands). They are very light and are easily identifiable as not of the quality that a multi-thousand dollar watch should use.

The more expensive replicas use aftermarket replacement bands that are sold for the legitimate model, or are used on related models of that watch. They are of higher-quality steel and use screws in the band as does a genuine Rolex. There is still a difference in weight if not appearance. These replacement bands feel stiff and a bit flimsy when compared to a real Rolex band.

Some of the Omega counterfeit bands are very close to the original, and have accurate pins when compared to the genuine issue bands. They are harder to tell apart from an initial inspection. On such models focus on other issues such as the case back and dial when trying to identify replicas.

5. The Dial: Fuzzy Printing?

Here's where that jeweler's loupe we told you to buy earns it's money. Look closely at the dial and date wheel (if present) through the loupe. The printing should be sharp and defined, not fuzzy around the edges or bleeding between letters. A genuine dial with sloppy printing would be rejected at the factory during inspection. The odds are that, unless the watch has been redialed, if it has irregular print quality it's a counterfeit.

There should be no dust on the surface of the dial, and absolutely no fingerprints. Contaminants such as hairs have been known to be found under counterfeit crystals. There's no quality control in the replica factories; each watch can exhibit a variety of subtle differences, including such things as contaminants and print quality.

6. Bezel Pearl: Inset or Ant Hill?

For Rolex sports models (Submariner and Sea-Dweller) the bezel pearl should be inset and luminous (glows in the dark). Current counterfeits have the bezel pearl applied so that it protrudes like a small ant hill; it also does not glow. Newer replicas have a bezel pearl more similar to the original yet it still does not sit flush to the bezel as a genuine bezel pearl should. Note that some people have replaced their replica bezel inserts with genuine ones (for a cost of around $100) which can eliminate this flaw.

7. General: Spell Check!

Many of these counterfeit watches are made in the Far East by people who's first language is not English. Because of this, several spelling errors have slipped into the final products and make determining if a watch is counterfeit very easy. Read carefully the dial and the case back. Check the spelling; don't assume that it's correct. We've seen spelling errors like "Eigtheem Jewels," "NIMITED EDITION," and "Made in Swiss," which make it obvious that the watch is not genuine.

These tips will help you quickly spot some obvious flaws in watches. Never rely on just one indicator that a watch might be counterfeit. Use your common sense and your specific knowledge of the watch to aid in the evaluation.

8. Sub-dials: Functional Chronograph?

When examining a chronograph, always try and work the pushers and examine the sub-dials in action. If a watch has a stopwatch function to and instead when you press the pusher it simply advances a hand by a tick it's probably really just a day/date/24-hour movement. All Rolex Daytona that should pass this test: when you press the top button the center second hand should begin to move. It shouldn't move unless the stopwatch function has been engaged.

Know how the genuine sub-dials is labeled: If you see a watch that has sub-dials labeled incorrectly then it may be a replica. An example of such a replica is a Rolex Daytona that has sub-dials with the days of the week.

9. Quartz Movements

Most high-end manufacturers don't use quartz movements on a majority of their watches. It's important that you research and find out which models they do make quartz versions of; it could save you a lot of money.   For example, there are no quartz versions of Roadster made by Cartier. If you see one with a ticking second hand then it's a replica (and probably a poor one at that. Most quartz replicas use inexpensive materials in their construction).

Be aware that Cartier does make quartz versions of its Divan model. Know how to tell the difference (automatic Divan's are labeled "Automatic" on the dial, quartz models have no such label). Knowing the product line can aid in your evaluation of a watch.

10. Luminosity

Most modern watches use a substance called LumiNova to provide the glow to the dial and hands that allows you to read the time in darkness. Replica watches normally have a poor quality luminous material applied compared to a genuine watch. The replica won't glow as brightly or as long when charged and viewed in a low light situation. It's also common that replicas will have missing luminous materials and not glow at all. Use a flashlight to "charge" a watch and observe the brightness of the dial and hands in the dark.

11. Bonus: Engraved Crown

Replicas are now attempting to emulate the engraved crown found at 6 o'clock on some Rolex models. Normally this crown is invisible to the naked eye (and is difficult even to spot with a 2.5x loupe). On some replicas the crown is so big it's easily spotted even from arms length. If you can see the

Replica with fake crown.

Buying Watches Online

Online auction houses such as eBay and Yahoo! Auctions have had a growing influence on the buying and selling of watches. Purchasing a watch online can be a fun experience if handled with care and a touch of skepticism. Just like any transaction where you're unable to see the goods except through the eyes of the seller, buying online is a process fraught with danger for the unsuspecting.

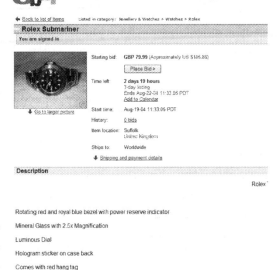

Ebay auctions are an easy way to buy and sell. It's also an easy way to rip an unsuspecting buyer off.

Warranties

Most high-end manufacturers don't honor the warranties of watches purchased from dealers on the Internet. This is to prevent gray market sales and to keep their distribution channels under control. To this end, most manufacturers' web sites will warn you about purchasing watches from online sources. Existing warranties for some manufacturers are also not transferable.

The safest way to buy any watch is from a reputable dealer for that brand. This may mean a slightly higher price than from online dealers, but you get the peace of mind knowing your purchase and warranty is honored by the manufacturer. Also the risk of unknowingly buying a counterfeit is negligible.

Buying from an Auction

When you come across the watch of your dreams on an online auction site, there are several things you need to do before getting too excited. Remember, all that you have to go by in evaluating the watch are:

1. Your knowledge of the watch in question.
2. The pictures the seller has posted.
3. The description of the watch he or she has provided.
4. The reputation of the seller.

Before you purchase any watch online make sure you're comfortable with each of these rules. Don't buy something with a wonderful description and pictures if the seller has a low feedback percentage. If you know the pictures of the watch are from the manufacturers' web site then be very wary of the listing. Balance all the rules against common sense before you buy.

Your Knowledge

The purpose of this book is to increase your general knowledge and awareness of the replicas on the market. But you should also research and learn as much as you can about the genuine watch before you buy. This means, when possible, visit your local dealer and get an opportunity to see the watch in person. There's no real substitute for seeing the genuine watch and getting an chance to handle it. Even if all you have to review are photographs, your personal experiences with the watch will aid in your decision making process.

> **" There are many online resources to turn to when evaluating a watch. "**

There are also many online resources to turn to in helping you evaluate a watch. Web site forums are an excellent source of information and support. Never abuse the privilege by excessively posting auction listings for evaluation to these forums. If you're sincere and request help, many forums will provide you with their informal opinion on a listing. Web forums like Timezone (www.timezone.com) and Paneristi (www.paneristi.com) are well known hang outs for experts on particular watch brands.

Be familiar with the manufacturer's web site. Visit the site and dig into the information that's posted there. Most of these web sites are light on information but have a variety of pictures available. They seem to feel its more important to have a flashy site than one that presents a list of features and data.

These sites are still wonderful tools to get an idea of the varieties of each model and to get a feel for the look of each watch. Plus many pictures from the manufacturer's web site are stolen and reused as actual item pictures in auctions. By being familiar with the manufacturer photographs (for example, Rolex always has their watches set to 10:10 and 31 seconds) you'll know what to look for.

The Seller's Pictures

It's very important to have good pictures available of a watch you're looking to buy. It states several things: that the seller is being open and honest about the sale by providing you a clear picture for inspection, and more importantly that the seller isn't trying to hide something by posting fuzzy pictures that obscure details.

This photo's poor quality can hide a host of ills.

Always look for pictures that show a watch at different angles. You want to see clearly the dial, case back, band or strap, and the clasp. By having clear pictures of these features it's easy to compare them to known genuine examples as well as look for flaws such as scratches, scrapes, and general wear.

Poor pictures provide you no assistance and actually hamper the sale by withholding information. If you have any doubts about a watch because of the pictures, tell the seller that you're interested in the item but you would like to see some additional photographs. One of the tricks you can use is to ask the seller to set the date or time to something specific to make sure that the pictures are actually of the watch they are selling.

Be aware that some unscrupulous people will use photos of other watches and represent them as their own. When this happens you're never sure of what you will actually get from the transaction; it could be a real watch, replica, or worse, nothing. Always feel free to ask the seller for additional pictures. His response will aid in making your choice.

My rule is that when the pictures are poor I'll pass on the auction. It's typically a sign of some kind of deception a seller unfamiliar with what they're selling. Still, if the watch is what you want, ask the seller for additional photographs to help you gather the information you need to make a decision.

The Seller's Description

The description the seller provides is your only source of detailed information about the watch in question. You should look for information about the condition of the watch, as well as exactly what comes with the purchase: i.e. boxes, papers, and paraphernalia. Details are a good sign that the seller knows what he has and finds it important that you, the potential buyer, have enough information to make an informed decision. I avoid auctions with terse, uninformative descriptions for lack of information.

When attempting to settle disputes over a transaction, sometimes buyers will refer to the item description when discussing misunderstandings or out and out fraud. Many disreputable sellers will try to hedge their bets by phrasing the description in a way where they can imply they were unaware of the authenticity of the watch. Common examples are:

"I bought the watch at an estate sale."
"It belonged to my grandfather who just passed."
"I got the watch as a gift from work."
"I'm selling it for a friend."
"I don't have the box or papers, but my jeweler said it was authentic."
"I can't vouch for the authenticity so bid accordingly."
"I'm no watch expert, but it looks real to me."
"This was my ex-boyfriend's watch and I just want to get rid of it."

And many more; the gist of it's the seller is unable or unwilling to fully vouch for the watch. This typically points to the fact that they are fully aware that the watch is a replica; they're just hoping you'll swallow the bait and ignore the caveat until it's time to complain. Avoid auctions that include any of these statements like the plague.

While even if the original box and paperwork is supplied with the watch, these things can (and have) been forged or faked. There is a market in replica Rolex boxes around the world; you can buy one for $25. While not an exact copy, they may pass as real in a photograph or to an unsuspecting buyer. Still, close ups of the paperwork (including the signed warranty card) are great. A copy of the sales receipt also adds credibility.

The Seller's Reputation

After all is said and done it all comes down to how well you can trust the other party in the transaction. You're purchasing a product sight unseen from a total stranger. You have to establish a certain level of trust with that individual to reduce your overall risk in the purchase.

eBay and most auction systems offer a method of feedback that provides a rating for a seller's previous transactions. This allows previous buyers to give the thumbs up or down on the way the seller handled the transaction and the quality of the goods compared to the description. This is a handy tool to gauge someone's past performance. But there is no guarantee that future transaction will be handled as previous ones have.

eBay has actually two ratings: the feedback rating which lists how many happy sellers they've dealt with, and a percentage that shows how many transactions they've had that have gone smoothly. A person with a high feedback number but a percentage in the low 70's means they've been busy but have had a lot of unsatisfied customers. Always look at both ratings when evaluating a seller.

Ebay gives you tools to research prior transactions of sellers and buyers. Use them before you bid.

Hackers and other family members may gain access to someone's auction account. By logging in and posting a listing for a product, they can use that seller's account and rating without the original user's knowledge. This means that guy with the 440 successful transactions may be, for this transaction, someone else with plans of ripping you off.

One way of reducing this risk is to view the detailed feedback information of the seller. Clicking on the seller's feedback number will allow you to view in detail the transactions they've been involved in. Look for some kind of recent change in reliability. Does the seller have plenty of good feedback until last month? This may be an indication of a hacker taking over.

Also look at whether the transactions are from buying or selling goods. A person that has bought 200 baseball cards in the past and is all of a sudden selling a $5,000 watch should be examined very closely. Don't let it be the only deciding factor; everyone has a first time for selling on eBay.

Higher ratings and sellers with storefronts are good indications that the person has something to lose by trying to cheat you. If a seller has a low rating (fewer than 20) he really has little to lose if you're unsatisfied. He doesn't have the built-up value to his account that someone who has hundreds of sales stands to see in jeopardy.

But even the big watch sellers online can be duped. I've seen several replica auctions from reputable sellers. The photographs reveal the problem usually. Their descriptions are detailed, but they are making the assumption the watch is real. Truly, this is where your knowledge and your objective examination of the listing really becomes important.

The Transaction

Before you buy or bid on a watch look carefully at the details of the listing itself. It will show the payment methods accepted, as well as the shipping charges you will incur. One of the tricks people use is to only accept money orders, wire transfers, or Western Union payments. All of these methods allow them to get the cash and give you no recourse later if you are unsatisfied. If possible, pay with a credit card, or even Paypal, which gives you some options to dispute the charge later if there is a problem.

Stay away from escrow services unless you are very familiar with the company. Escrow services act as a third party in the transaction. They hold the buyer's money until the buyer receives the item. Once the buyer has inspected the item and is satisfied the escrow company releases the cash to the seller.

There are several scams that involve you sending your money to an escrow service that is in reality just a vehicle to get your credit card information, or to take your money. Escrow handled properly is a good way in dealing with large transactions where a lot of risk is involved. Frankly, if you're spending $20,000 on a Patek Philippe it's probably worth the plane ticket to meet the seller at an authorized dealer and handle the transaction face to face.

Shipping is something to be concerned with as well; if the seller is in a foreign country be aware that there may be trouble in getting the watch through customs. Customs will want to charge you fees for importing the watch into the country. Buying from someone with experience in providing the proper forms for customs can aid in speeding up this process.

Buying from a foreign seller also involves higher shipping costs. Always insist on the watch being shipped via EMS, or some other carrier such as FedEx, that can provide a tracking number and insurance for the package. This gives you a way of following the shipment to your doorstep.

Buying from a seller in the same country is the easiest way to deal with this process as shipping is greatly simplified. I prefer to use US Postal System's Priority Mail as it's relatively inexpensive and can provide tracking and insurance. One of the nice features of eBay is you can generate the necessary postage directly from eBay and Paypal. This makes shipping a package easy and aids in the paper trail.

It's Here!

Once you receive the watch, open the package carefully and inspect the goods. Have your moment of satisfaction and excitement, but then move onto making sure you received what you paid for. This means look at the watch in detail; inspect the case back and dial. Is it the proper color dial? Do all the functions work properly? Does it wind well and does the crown screw down tightly? This is your best opportunity to find fault with the watch.

Hopefully the watch is what you wanted and you can happily leave positive feedback for the seller on the auction site. Be sure to ask the seller to leave you feedback as well. This benefits both parties by raising your ratings.

If you have a problem with the watch, or the transaction, immediately e-mail or contact the seller and politely describe what the problem is. Perhaps they forgot to ship the paperwork, or maybe the watch doesn't meet the description on the auction. Your first step should be to try to work something out with the seller. It could very well be an honest mistake on their part and something they'll work to correct.

If for some reason you're unable to contact or can't reach a settlement with the seller you can contact the auction house and have them attempt to mediate a solution. When all else fails it's time to contact your credit card company and dispute the transaction. Remember to leave negative feedback that describes the problem and the lack of resolution.

Whatever you do, don't just sit and stew. This process is something best dealt with quickly while all the details are still fresh.

Non-Auction Purchases

When buying from an individual or an online dealer you should follow closely the rules laid out for auction purchases. The four golden rules apply; examine all the information you're given before you make a purchase. Look closely at the pictures posted for the watch. I seldom consider purchasing anything where I can't see the exact item I'll be receiving. This means sites or sellers that use stock photographs will not get my business. It's too easy to mislead without this critical piece of data.

I also read over several times the description of the watch. Never feel shy in asking questions of the seller. Ask them if they're the first owner of the watch, and if so, where did they buy it. Ask them to show you the watch in different positions so you can examine it in detail. Remember, it's you that will be taking the risk in this transaction, so go into the process armed with as much information as you can.

I've had the most luck buying from sites like Timezone, where the community is tight and self-policing. There are other sites and dealers that offer good communication and good product, but as anywhere online there is no guarantee that previous performance will be duplicated in future transactions. It's definitely a situation where the buyer must beware. Hopefully we've given you the tools to help you make informed and deliberate decisions.

Selling Watches Yourself

All the tips listed above should be applied to any watch you sell yourself. That means provide good close-up pictures and detailed descriptions of the watch and it's condition. Respond quickly and politely to any questions asked by potential buyers. You too can build a reputation as an honest online seller.

I'd add one additional thing to think about as a seller: No matter how friendly a buyer is, he's only as good as his money. Don't let someone make promises to handle a transaction outside the boundaries of your normal methods. This means if you have your watch listed on eBay, complete the transaction on eBay, no matter how attractive the buyer makes the alternative sound. Usually people try to avoid the auction houses because they are bound by their rules and policies. eBay gives you alternatives if a transaction handled by them goes bad.

Some sellers want you to end your auction so you can avoid paying listing fees. In reality they may be trying to eliminate your options by removing eBay as a "traffic cop" in the transaction. Don't do it; use the auction web sites and forums as a mediator in your sales.

Replicas and Retail Don't Mix

This chapter is designed for retail sellers, of both new and used watches. It's not designed as a criminal education seminar; don't try these at home! These scenarios are just examples of the way that replicas can be used to fool unsuspecting and unprepared salespeople.

Why do I need to know about replica watches?

"Why should I care about counterfeit merchandise? After all we never BUY watches from our customers; therefore we're not vulnerable to losses."

Actually, this is untrue; whenever you let customers handle your merchandise you are opening yourself to various forms of fraud. One of the most obvious is the simple swapping of the real product with a counterfeit copy. Some of the recent counterfeit watches are close enough to the originals to fool a person who performs only a cursory examination of the watch.

The Upstanding Businessman

The Setup

A well dressed, well groomed businessman approaches your counter at your upscale jewelry boutique. As is your habit, you glance at his watch to try and judge his potential spending habits. He's wearing a gold Rolex President; you see it peeking out of the sleeve of his suit. At once you mentally categorize him as a very strong potential customer.

He greets you amiably and then begins to look at the watches in your case. He seems to be eyeing a particular Rolex quite closely: a stainless steel Daytona. You volunteer to show him the watch and you pull it from the cabinet and place it on a display card. The gentleman picks up the watch and begins to examine it closely.

> *You absent-mindedly put the Daytona back in the cabinet. You've just been taken for $10,000.*

Just then another man enters the store and approaches your counter. He loudly declares he's shopping for a gold Rolex Submariner and wants to know your price on it immediately. You unfortunately don't have one in stock, so you turn for a second to look up the price. While this new customer is holding your attention the original customer receives a call on his cell phone, appears preoccupied. He puts the watch down on the counter, waves at you, and walks out the front door.

Once he's gone your new customer no longer seems as interested in the Submariner, but waits for you to give him the price and announces that he can find it cheaper on the Internet. He walks out, leaving you a bit bewildered and flustered. You absent-mindedly put the Daytona back into the cabinet.

You've just been taken for a $10,000 watch.

The Trap

There were three people involved in this deception. One was the original customer who lulled you into a false sense of security with his quiet display of wealth. You assumed, by his dress and demeanor, that he might be a potential customer with means, and therefore you assigned to him a certain low level of risk. Because of that false sense of trust you determine he is safe to turn your back on while he handles an expensive piece of jewelry.

The second perpetrator is of course the new customer. He is being loud and drawing more attention to himself for the sole purpose of pulling the eyes off the first customer. You subconsciously assign this person a higher level of risk, and his demand for immediate attention forces you to make a quick decision. You draw upon your assumed level of trust with the first customer and leave him to his own devices "for a second" while you deal with the new customer.

As soon as your attention is fixed on the new customer the "businessman" begins the swindle. He swaps quickly the real Daytona with a very accurate counterfeit. The counterfeit doesn't have to be spot on, as you won't be examining it closely until he's gotten clean away. He has time also to defeat any security methods you might have. The reason for this is that your store has been "cased" by the third person involved in the theft.

The previous day this person came in as a customer and asked to examine the exact same watch the "businessman" asked to see. During this trip the third criminal carefully checked the watch for any security tags, as well as examining the camera layout in the building to determine the best angle for the "businessman" to stand while performing the swap. All this can be done while cheerfully talking to the salesperson and taking mental notes of the environment. Now this third person acts as the "getaway" driver for the "businessman". She's waiting in the parking lot with the car running.

While you're looking up the price on the gold Submariner the "businessman" casually swaps the watch and signals the driver with a press of the walkie-talkie feature on his phone. This signals the driver to call the "businessman's" cell phone. He picks up the phone and begins an imaginary business conversation with a customer or work. He uses key words to help the driver understand the situation in the store. If you had become suspicious then he'd signal to the driver that the sting was off and to drive away, or to perform whatever secondary operation was required. Otherwise the driver would have the car ready and the passenger side door unlocked.

As the fictional phone conversation continued the "businessman" would absent-mindedly walk off towards the door. A few steps taken and he'd remember the Daytona and grab your attention and put it onto the counter top. With a wave he's off; your trusted customer with a valid excuse for leaving: the phone call. Since he has a valid reason for ending the transaction you don't feel it necessary to check the watch right then. After all you have your hands full with the Submariner guy.

Once outside the "businessman" gets into the driver's car and they pull off at a normal pace. They've just scored a $10,000 watch which they can change the serial number on and resell out of the country for a substantial amount of money. All for an hour's worth of work. You have no way of tracing them unless someone happened to catch the plates of the car. Even then, there are ways to make this an invalid way of tracing the criminals.

Meanwhile, his job done, the Submariner customer really is there only to buy time for his co-conspirators. The longer it's before you check the Daytona the higher the chance of his friends being able to get clean away. You have no way of tracing the fact that the two customers are involved together, so there's no reason to suspect him even if you notice the watch is counterfeit. His job is to get you flustered and focused on him, and in turn, force you make instinctual decisions instead of rational ones. He walks out confidently, leaving you to wonder why he bothered coming in.

Now finally you turn to the Daytona on the countertop. If the second customer did his job you are so preoccupied with his performance that you give the watch only a quick glance. After all you've seen it every day for two months. You carefully put it back into the cabinet and then go off to your daily routine. It might be days before someone notices a discrepancy with the watch. On some watches it may only be determined that it's counterfeit when the serial number doesn't match the inventory forms.

This trick can be done with any high end stainless steel watch, be it Rolex, Cartier or Franck Muller for example. I say stainless steel because it's easy to match the weight and appearance of a stainless steel watch compared to a high end solid gold watch. Most gold counterfeit watches are plated. There is a significant weight difference between the solid gold and gold plated watches that would be noticeable even by a distracted salesperson. Stainless watches are so close in weight that it's not a noticeable factor that will reveal the scam.

> **" This trick can be done with any high-end stainless steel watch: Rolex, Cartier or Franck Muller "**

Other factors go into making the swap successful. The counterfeit watch has to match the appearance of the original. This is one of the reasons the third criminal "cases" the store the day before. They check the dial and band of the watch to make sure they have an exact match on the counterfeit.

The counterfeit also cannot be too warm. If worn on the wrist a watch absorbs over time the heat of the body of the wearer. This would be detectable if the watch was body temperature that the salesperson was putting away. To avoid this issue the counterfeit watch is not worn but kept in a pouch or secret pocket. This reduces the body heat the watch absorbs. It may be kept in a storage box until right before the businessman enters the store.

Initial appearance is also important. The counterfeit watch has to be in a condition to match the original. This means it must be free of scratches and clean, as well as sport all tags and protective tape that the original had. The "casing" of the watch can reveal all that needs to be known about the original watch's state.

These factors: your trust of the businessman, the appearance of the watch, the manner of the businessman's leaving, the distraction tactics of the second customer, and the reconnaissance of the third criminal the day before, all lead up to a potentially successful robbery in broad daylight. Sales staff need to be aware of not only the risk of leaving high end jewelry with a customer, but also the quality of counterfeit watches in today's market.

The Solo Artist

The Setup

In this situation a customer with shopping bags walks into your boutique. She's very interested in one of your Cartier Roadsters for her husband. She's got her arms full of bags and sets them down heavily on the floor. It's the holiday season so this seems perfectly natural to you. You greet her with a smile and pull out your selection of Roadsters for her to examine.

She seems torn between two different models, and has you show her how to work the clasp. She asks you questions about the watch; and during the conversation slips in comments about her personal life. She seems very personable, and enjoys telling a story about her 6-year old and her pearl necklace at home. All the while she's clumsily working at the bracelet on the Cartier. All of a sudden the watch slips out of her hands and falls into the shopping bag at her feet.

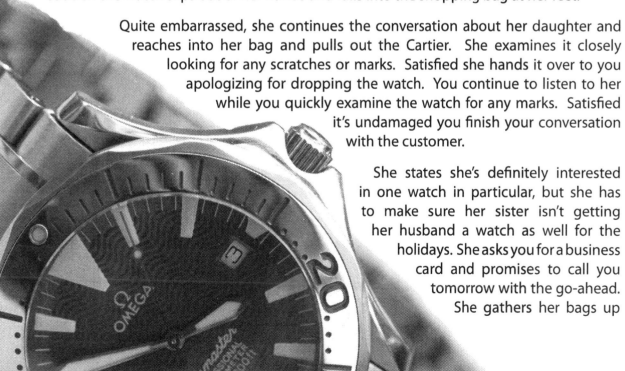

Quite embarrassed, she continues the conversation about her daughter and reaches into her bag and pulls out the Cartier. She examines it closely looking for any scratches or marks. Satisfied she hands it over to you apologizing for dropping the watch. You continue to listen to her while you quickly examine the watch for any marks. Satisfied it's undamaged you finish your conversation with the customer.

She states she's definitely interested in one watch in particular, but she has to make sure her sister isn't getting her husband a watch as well for the holidays. She asks you for a business card and promises to call you tomorrow with the go-ahead. She gathers her bags up and heads for the door. You carefully put the watch back in the cabinet and continue on with your business.

You've been taken this time for nearly $4,000.

The Trap

The particular scam is done by only one person, relying on the sales person being busy or distracted. It will almost never be done on a slow day or when there isn't other activity in the store.

The crook prepares in advance by taking a replica of the watch he or she wishes to steal and attaching it to the inside of a large paper store bag with double sided tape. It has to stick to the sides so it can be easily grabbed when needed. Next, the bag itself is stuffed with a soft fluffy material, like scarves or sweaters. This is done to muffle the sound of the watch and to envelope it when it falls into the bag; it can't sit on the top when it lands where it might be spotted.

This scam relies almost totally on the risk that a salesperson assigns to the watch being dropped. If the inspection of the swapped watch is done quickly it might seem to be the correct watch and the potential risk seems to be low.

Also, if the salesperson has a lot of customers, like around the Christmas shopping season, they may set the risk level low because of the amount of inconvenience it would be to check more in detail with several customers waiting to be served. After all they got the watch back with no scratches.

Lessons Learned

The primary lessons to be learned from the above two examples is that one should never take for granted any unusual situation. Any situation that takes you out of your normal practices is a potential risk for fraud.

As a store there should be detailed policies for handling watches, and those policies should be followed to the letter. I've been in stores where a drivers license is required to handle items from the case, and other stores where you're handed an expensive watch and the sales person is distracted or disinterested. In both cases the employee, not the store, is enforcing a certain level of security.

Current replicas are good enough to fool people doing quick examinations. They weigh the same as a genuine watch, and in some cases are nearly identical in appearance. By knowing what to look for both in the watch and the customer you can avoid potential theft or fraud.

Know Your Product

One weakness in larger stores is that the sales people aren't familiar in depth with all the watches currently being sold. This may be because of the number of watch models sold, or because salespeople are assigned particular brands and have little exposure to other watches. This is potentially a problem because salespeople are unfamiliar with the look and feel of the inventory.

I suggest that once a month all the salespeople come in after hours and have an opportunity to handle the merchandise. Have them learn the way the watches look: the dial, the case, the weight and feel. Have them wind the watches, work the pushers. This will allow them to gain a level of familiarity with the watches that will serve them well when dealing with customers.

Know Your Customers

Perception is very important when handling transactions between customers. When you're handed the watch back, take a second to point out some salient features while you secretly examine the watch. Point out the detail on the dial while you examine it for flaws. You can make your examination a lesson for the customer on the details of the watch.

Also, never make assumptions about any customer. In today's world a millionaire can just as easily walk in wearing a T-shirt and jeans sporting a Casio. The opposite holds true as well; a replica watch on the wrist can from a distance appear real, giving a customer the appearance of being wealthy. If you have to make an assumption about a customer, pretend each one is a secret shopper sent in to spy on you by management. Make sure they're happy, but be on guard for them to test you!

Scams

Most of the scams practiced today rely on several things: distraction, deception, and speed. If any of these elements fail, the scam itself will most likely not be successful. It's the salespersons job to be the obstacle between the scammer and a successful heist.

The distraction element is important. When salesperson is distracted from a customer it opens up a variety of ways that customer can take advantage of this lapse in supervision. This can vary from price switching to product exchanges. Always be careful and keep an eye on the customer. If you're forced to be called away, collect the merchandise politely explain that you'll be right back. Never, under any circumstances, leave product with an unsupervised customer. Even if they're not planning some evil deed, a customer can damage a watch if they're unsure how to operate its functions.

Deception, in this case, is typically swapping a replica watch with a genuine one. This means that if the distraction attempt was successful the perpetrator has an opportunity to exchange watches. At this point there is an inherent reliance on the salesperson's lack of knowledge or attention. Handing back a high quality Rolex replica is less risky than a cheap Chinatown copy to the scammer. But either will get them busted equally if the salesperson notices the difference.

Speed is the final element of a successful scam. Given enough time to thoroughly examine a watch even the most distracted salesperson will eventually notice something is wrong. The key to the crook is to get in and get out before there is time or even an inclination to perform an examination. That is why it's important to examine the watch immediately when you are handed back the product.

Enforcement

If you do spot an instance of fraud, make sure there is a company policy in place on how to handle it safely and efficiently. This is an important step that should be handled in advance. There should be a way to alert the other staff to the situation, as well as securing the merchandise and the customer. This is important for the safety of all involved. If it seems to be a dangerous situation do the safe thing and don't interfere. Note any key features of the crook so that you can give a good description to the police. Your safety is more important than any piece of jewelry.

Assigning Risk

After reading this section it may seem that every customer potentially is out to get you; this is not the case. The chance of fraud is greatest only in unusual situations. This means cases where you are forced to divide your attention, or something strange happens while the customer is handling the watch. With normal practices, such as never looking away and examining the goods on return, most customers are no threat to the store. The biggest risk comes into play when you are forced to behave in a manner you aren't prepared for. The purpose of this book is to aid you in knowing what to look for.

Using This Book

After reading this chapter, the best way to use this book is to read carefully through the Spotter's Guide section for the brands you carry. It's designed in a way that is tailor-made for the retail sector; each watch lists clues and flaws that can quickly be detected by a surface examination. Read each description carefully; if possible handle a genuine watch of each model while you're reading the book to aid you in spotting the differences for each piece.

Memorization of the flaws to look for is quite important. It's not wise to take the time to go to the back room to peruse the book while you have a customer waiting. It's also not a good idea to leaf through the book in front of the customer. Taking 15 minutes a day to go over a particular model and comparing in detail to a genuine watch is a good exercise in aiding building quick observational skills.

Caveat

Remember that this book is a guide and not the final word. There are so many vagaries and variations in each brand and model that is impossible to detail them all in a single book. Use your common sense and the tools presented here in this book to assist your intuition and observational skills in learning how to assign risk.

Frequently Asked Questions

I've noticed a need for a list of questions and answers for those people new to replica and watches. The following section covers many of the main points of interest as they are related to genuine and replica watches. I'm always on the lookout for more content for the FAQ; if you have something you'd like clarified or points you'd like to see added please feel free to contact me at *faq@chronosafe.com*.

General Questions

Q: What is a replica watch?

A: A replica watch is a functional or partially functional copy of an original watch design of a famous manufacturer. In my opinion, only a watch that doesn't function as a timepiece (such as a prop) should be defined by the term "fake."

Q: What are "Swiss" replicas?

A: The term "Swiss" refers to the quality of the watch, usually indicating that the movement is made in Switzerland. This movement is typically made by ETA (http://www.eta.ch). "Swiss" quality replicas are some of the best in the industry, and are usually more accurate in their appearance.

"Swiss" replicas tend to cost more than other examples, giving their manufacturers more leeway to use more expensive materials in their construction. Swiss replicas will use sapphire crystals and higher quality dials. **There are no replicas made in Switzerland; repeat, there are no replicas made in Switzerland.** The Swiss authorities are very protective of their industries. Anyone who claims replicas are made in Switzerland is probably attempting to deceive you.

Note: "Swiss", "Japanese", and "Asian," in reference to replicas are broad terms covering a lot of ground. A "Swiss" watch may be of lower quality than a "Japanese" example; since there is no quality control in the manufacturing of replicas, quality varies greatly from watch to watch.

Q: What are "Japanese" replicas?

A: The term "Japanese" replica refers to the quality and origin of the movement in the watch. "Japanese" movements are usually of lesser quality than the Swiss movements, but are also less expensive. This means the overall cost of the watch is less than Swiss replicas. "Japanese" replicas also typically use inferior materials in their construction compared to the original watch.

"Japanese" replicas are more common, and are easier to spot because of the shortcuts taken in their construction. They will use sapphire or even mineral glass crystals, and typically a poorer attention to detail than the higher-end models.

Q: What are "Asian" replicas?

A: "Asian" replicas are made of very inferior materials. They are easy to spot as replicas because they are lighter and flimsier than the original. "Asian" replicas are common items in Chinatown, and can be purchased for around $30.

"Asian" replicas are what many people think of when the term "replica watch" is brought up in conversation. They are cheap imitations of the original, mass-produced for tourists. These watches will use poor quality pot metal cases plated over to imitate stainless steel. Also glass and plastic crystals are common. Even plastic parts in the movement have been known. There's little difficulty in spotting a replica of this quality; they don't look like five thousand dollar watches.

Q: What is "triple" and "single" wrapped gold?

A: Solid gold is too expensive a material to make replicas from. Most "gold" replicas instead use some type of gold plating to emulate a real gold watch. Normal plating puts a single layer of about 2-4 microns of gold plating on a watch; this is enough to give a gold look to the watch, but the thin plating wears off over time.

"Triple" wrapped watches simply means that this plating process is done three times, giving a very thick coating of gold to the watch. This coating is thick enough that watches with "triple" wrapped gold plating can pass for solid gold watches in some tests. This coating also resists fading better than more lightly plated watches.

Another theory is that this term is a marketing ploy developed by replica dealers online. There is no evidence that this multiple plating is done; the best guess is that a thicker coating of gold is used on the higher-end watches than on cheaper models.

Q: Is all stainless steel the same in replica construction?

A: No, some cheaper Asian replicas actually use stainless steel plating over a pot metal core. This can wear off just like gold plating can. It tends to be very shiny and looks "fake." Some Japanese replicas use a cheaper quality of stainless steel in their manufacturing process. Most Swiss replicas use 440 Stainless, which is the same quality of metal that some of the original manufacturers use. Not using the proper materials can mean that the replica can feel light in comparison to the original. Some low-end replica manufacturers use weights inside the case to try and match the original watch.

Q: Should my metal watch band have pins or screws in it?

A: It depends on the model, but most original watches with metal bands have screws in the last links of the band to allow it to be sized for the wearer. Some early Rolex models used rivets, but all of the current models have screws in the band. Cheaper replicas use pins to hold the links together because it's less expensive.

Omega is a manufacturer that uses pins in their bands.

Q: What is the difference between mineral glass and sapphire?

A: First of all, the crystal is the clear part of the watch that protects the face from the elements. On some models this is slightly convex (like a magnifying glass), on other models it sits slightly projecting from the case. This covering or "crystal" is usually made out of several types of materials:

Mineral Glass – This is a specially treated glass that is more resistant than normal glass to scratches. It can still be scratched with a sharp object like a knife or a razor blade. With careful wear you can get a long life out of a mineral glass crystal.

Sapphire – Artificial sapphire is used in the higher-end replicas, and on original watches such as Rolex, Patek Philippe, and Rado. Having a hardness rating just slightly under diamonds sapphire crystals are usually impervious to scratches. Because of their hardness they can shatter if subjected to hard blows. This is the recommended material for a crystal.

Q: What is a crown?

A: The "crown" of a watch is the knob that is used to wind or set the time. A typical crown on an automatic watch can do several functions: set the time, wind the watch, set the date and day. Some watches have multiple crowns if there are additional functions that need to be controlled.

Note: Rolex uses a one piece crown with the Rolex logo at the end. There are different dots or bars under the crown that indicate the type of movement and functions that the crown will perform.

Cheap Rolex replicas will have a two-piece crown, with the emblem actually glued onto the end of a generic crown. These are noticeable by the lip around the glued-on emblem.

Note: Some crowns have gems instead of emblems at their end. Counterfeit gems have a glass-like quality to them and can typically be easily identified.

Q: What is an anti-reflective coating (AR coating)?

A: Some manufacturers coat the inside and or outside of the crystal of their watches with a thin film that cuts down on the reflections visible when viewing the dial. This anti-reflective film sometimes gives a slight blue tint to the crystal.

Manufacturers like Breitling, Panerai, and Omega use this coating extensively through their product line. The effect of the coating is that the watch crystal appears to be invisible at certain viewing angles. Also the watch is viewable in outdoor setting where without the coating the glare would make reading the dial difficult.

Note: A missing anti-reflective coating is one of the easiest way to spot a counterfeit. Move the watch around and view it from different angles. If the crystal remains glossy and reflective from various angles then it does not have the coating. This is great way to spot fake Panerais and Breitlings as they are great proponents of the coating.

Q: Are counterfeit watches waterproof?

A: Since there is no quality control in the making of a replica, there is no way to determine if an individual watch will be waterproof. Some replicas may pass a pressure test, while the next watch made by the same builder may fail. These watches may have markings indicating they are water resistant but remember, these are counterfeit watches. The markings are lies.

Q: Are replica watches legal?

A: Replicas of an original model watch are considered counterfeit. Like any counterfeit item they are not legal. Rolex and other manufacturers are actively working to eliminate replica manufacturers. It's illegal to sell, trade, or transport counterfeit goods.

Q: What is a deployant clasp?

A: A deployant clasp is a metal clasp that typically is fitted to a leather strap. This clasp closes the watchband instead of using a traditional tang and buckle. Deployants are easy to open and close with one hand and usually allow you to adjust the watch strap to finer degree than a normal tang and buckle.

Movement Questions

Q: What is a watch movement?

A: The movement of a watch is the mechanical parts that keeps the time and causes the hands of the watch to move. There are several different types of movements, but usually three are used in replicas: quartz, manual and automatic.

Q: What is a quartz movement?

A: A quartz movement is a movement that relies on the vibrations of a quartz crystal to keep time. Powered usually by a battery, quartz movements are accurate and cheap to make. Many of the watches that replicas emulate don't use quartz movements. This means that if a replica has a quartz movement it's not going to function like the original watch. Quartz watches have a "ticking" motion to the second hand, which usually gives it away as a replica, since most original watches have a "sweeping" hand.

Q: What does the number of jewels in a movement mean?

A: "Jewels" are usually synthetic rubies used in a movement to reduce friction. Most movements are use at least 17 jewels in their design, at critical points of wear. Additional jewels may be used when the movement has additional functions, such as acting as a chronograph or a date wheel.

These additional jewels do not add to the accuracy of the movement; they are there to reduce the wear for the parts of the additional components. The Rolex 3135 movement, used in the Submariner, uses 31 jewels in its design. The ETA 2836-2, used in many Submariner replicas, has the same functionality and uses 25 jewels. ETA does not make a movement that is used in replicas with 27 jewels as some web sites claim.

Again, additional jewels do not increase accuracy, they simply reduce wear which can extend the life of the movement.

Q: What is an automatic movement?

A: An automatic movement is also sometimes called a "self-winding" movement. It uses the movement of your arm through the normal activity of your day to wind the watch. Usually there is a weight set on a pivot called a rotor that rocks and swings back and forth with the rhythm of your movements. This swinging winds the main spring of the watch, just as if you were manually winding it over time.

The higher quality replica watches will typically use an automatic movement since this is the movement used in the original watch they are emulating. Automatic movements are not as accurate as quartz movements, and are more expensive.

Q: What is a manual movement?

A: Manual movements are also sometimes called "hand wound." They are the traditional movements that require human effort to wind the crown in order to power the watch. Winding the crown causes a spring to tighten inside the watch. Over the course of the day the spring releases its energy in order to move the gears of the watch. When the spring loses all of its energy the watch stops running. Some manual watches have a "Power Reserve" that indicates how many hours of energy the spring has remaining.

Q: What is a "sweeping" second hand?

A: All Swiss replicas and some automatic Japanese replicas use a movement that has a sweeping second hand. This simply means that instead of "ticking" once per second, the sweeping second hand moves several times a second, giving the appearance of a smooth, constant movement. Quartz movements don't exhibit this feature.

Q: What is a chronograph?

A: A chronograph is a set of small dials on a watch that acts as a stop-watch to record the passing of time for an event. Most chronographs have three dials that record: seconds, minutes and hours (24 hour clock). These functions can be controlled and set from the crown and other buttons on the side of the watch. On some replicas the movement used does not have real chronograph function, but instead acts as a date indicator. So the three dials will function as: day, date, 24 hours. This is an obvious give-away that a watch may be a replica.

Q: What is a chronometer?

A: Officially, a chronometer is a movement tested for accuracy by the Contrôle Officiel Suisse des Chronomètres (COSC), a Swiss organization that certifies watch movements. This certification is given to those movements that pass a series of test that prove the reliability and accuracy of that movement in a variety of conditions. These certifications are awarded only to those manufacturers who submit their movements for evaluation. Rolex, Panerai, Omega, Breitling, and Tag Heuer are some of the companies who seek COSC certification. Rolex, who certifies all their movements, makes up 60% of those movements tested each year.

Q: What is a "hacking" movement?

A: Many high quality automatic movements, like those used in Rolex replicas, will stop the second hand while you are setting the time. This allows people to synchronize their watch with other watches. This is called a "hacking" function.

Q: What is a sub-dial?

A: On certain watches there are additional indicators on the dial for specific functions. As an example, on a Rolex Daytona there are 3 smaller "dials" on the main dial face that indicate seconds, elapsed minutes and elapsed hours. These other dials are typically controlled with additional buttons on the side of the watch called "pushers". A Rolex Daytona has two pushers: one resets the elapsed hands to 0, and the other pusher starts the tracking of time by the sub-dials.

Q: What is the dial of watch?

A: The dial is also called the "face" of the watch. It's the surface of the watch that displays the numerals or markers for the hours and minutes. Some watches have very complex faces, while others are simple and elegant.

There are different quality levels of dials: ink printed dials; laser printed dials and genuine dials. The Swiss replicas use laser printed or genuine dials while higher-grade Japanese replicas use laser printed dials. The lower-end replicas use ink printed dials. Laser and genuine dials are the sharpest, while ink dials can be fuzzy.

Q: What is a pusher?

A: A pusher is a button on the side of a watch case used to activate the stopwatch function. Additional pushers can be used to reset the stop watch function or perform other duties that need to be manually initiated.

Q: What is a "Bi-compax" and "Tri-compax" movement?

A: Bi-compax indicates that there are two working sub-dial functions on a particular movement, usually located at the 3 and 9 o'clock positions. Tri-compax means there are three sub-dials on a movement. These sub-dials are usually activated by a pusher or button on the case. The Rolex Daytona is an example of a watch with a tri-compax movement.

Q: What is a case back?

A: The case back of watch is the cover on the back that protects the movement. Rolex uses a screw-down case back, which means you need a tool to help unscrew the cover to expose the movement for servicing. Other watches have a transparent panel in the case back to allow you to view the movement during normal operations. Note that genuine Rolexes will NEVER have a transparent case back, nor will they (with certain exceptions, such as the Sea-Dweller) ever have any engraving on the back.

Q: What is a watch band link?

A: The average watch band is actually made up of several segments that are held together by screws or pins. These segments are called links. These links are often made up of several segments that are held together to offer flexibility. Rolex uses dowels and screws to hold the links of their bands together. The band can be "sized" to fit a particular wrist by removing links near the clasp.

Q: What is a spring bar?

A: In order to connect a watch band or strap to the actual watch head, many manufacturers use a device called a "spring bar." The spring bar is a short bar that has spring-loaded tips. This allows the bar to 'shorten" temporarily in order to fit between the lugs of the watch.

Q: What the holes in the side of a Rolex case for?

A: Older Rolexes have holes in the side of the case that allow an owner to push a pin-like device, called a spring bar tool, through the lugs in order to remove the spring bar.

Q: What are gold hallmarks?

A: Watches made out of solid gold normally will have a mark or symbol certifying that the gold is genuine and of high quality. These marks are called "hallmarks" and are typically located on the back of the case.

Q: What is "blued steel"?

A: The process of chemically treating metal and subjecting it to heat in order to temper or strengthen that metal can also cause it to turn a blue color. The actual metal itself changes color; it's not painted or plated. Many gun manufacturers use this process, as do watch makers when fashioning hands on a watch.

Many replicas emulate this process by painting the hands on certain watches a blue color. This color is quite bright and is easily identified as painting instead of the true process.

Q: What does the "750" engraved on the back of my watch mean?

A: An engraving that reads "750" typically indicates that the watch is made with 18k gold. The 750 represents the amount of pure gold in the manufacture of the case. Solid gold (24k) is rated at 1000, but is too soft to be used in making watch parts. It's mixed with an amount of other materials in order to strengthen the metal as well as provide a variety of colors

If your case has the 750 mark and others around it (such as "18k") it means the case "should" be gold. If the case is stainless steel instead, it's an indication that the replica manufacturer plates this model when they want a "gold" version, and are too cheap to make a version for the stainless steel (non-gold) variant.

Q: What is a display or exhibition back?

A: A display back is a case that has a window on the back of the watch that allows people to view the movement in action. On most replicas this is a dead give-away to it being a counterfeit since the movement it shows is not the same movement as the genuine item. Replica movements are typically unfinished and rough in appearance in comparison to the original movements which are decorated.

Q: What is a mainspring?

A: The mainspring is used in any mechanical watch to store energy. This energy is released over time and used to move the gears of the watch in normal use. The mainspring gains energy whenever you wind your watch, or if it uses an automatic movement, whenever you walk and swing your arms.

Quartz movements don't have a mainspring; their energy is stored in a battery used to vibrate a quartz crystal.

Q: What is a bezel?

A: The bezel of a watch is the ring of metal (or other substance) that surrounds the crystal. This ring can be plain or embellished (like the fluted bezel of some Rolexes), or can serve a function such as the bezel of a Rolex Submariner which acts as a dive timer.

Note: On some watches the bezel is fixed in position, while other watches have bezels that rotate clockwise or in both directions. Watches with smaller bezels tend to appear to have larger crystals.

Q: What is a rotor?

A: Automatic movements are self-winding because there is a device called a "rotor" that rotates on a pivot. This rotation is caused by the natural movement of your arms. As you walk the forces generated by you swinging your arms causes this rotor to spin around a central hub. This energy is transferred to the main spring which in effect "winds" the watch.

Rolex Questions

Q: What is Quick Set date and time?

A: The quick set on a Rolex allows you to set the date wheel on the watch without having to manipulate the time. Without Quick Set you are forced to rotate the hands of the watch through the normal hours of the day. This means if you need to advance the date by five days you would have to rotate the hour hand ten times around the dial! In order to avoid this quick set allows you to independently rotate the date wheel by pulling the crown out to a certain position.

Double quick set watches allow you to adjust both the date and day.

Q: My watch says "T<25" at the bottom of the dial instead of "Swiss Made". Is this wrong?

A: Some Rolexes used the T<25 to indicate the millirads of radiation given off by the tritium used to make the hands and dial glow. This is a normal Rolex marking for watches made before 1998. Models after that date were made with a non-radioactive substance called LumiNova, and are marked "Swiss Made."

LumiNova normally has a greenish glow while tritium glows white.

Q: Where is the serial number and model number on my watch?

A: Most Rolexes have the serial number engraved at the 6 o'clock position on the case in the spot that the band attaches to the watch (called the lugs). The model number is engraved under the 12 o'clock position.

Rolexes don't normally have engravings on the back of the case (notable exceptions are the COMEX Submariner, Sea-Dweller, and certain ladies models). This is usually an indication the watch is a replica.

Note: Some watches have the serial number engraved on the watch band or case back. Many high-end Swiss replicas have all the engravings and markings in the proper place.

Q: What is a cyclops?

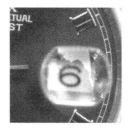

A: Some Rolex models have a magnification device over the date called a "cyclops." This small lens makes the date easier to view at a glance. One of the weaknesses of Rolex replicas is that the cyclops does not magnify the date sufficiently; on a real Rolex the date should nearly fill the cyclops lens.

Q: Is there a crown on the crystal of a Rolex?

A: On newer (2002+) watches Rolexes has started to use a very small, nearly imperceptible crown etched at the 6 o'clock position on the crystal. This crown is an anti-counterfeiting device designed to make determining authenticity easier.

Several replica manufacturers have copied this crown with varying levels of success. If the crown is visible with the naked eye then it's most likely on a replica. The crown should only be visible with a loupe; even then it's difficult to   pick out.

Note that not all new Rolexes yet have this etching, and that it does not apply to watches made before this was implemented.

Q: What is a bezel pearl?

A: On Rolex Submariners and Sea-Dwellers there is a small pearl-like marker at the 12 o'clock position on the bezel insert. This marker is used to aid in reading the position of the bezel in low light conditions. The bezel pearl should glow in the dark when charged, just like the hour markers on the dial.

Many replicas have an incorrect bezel pearl, which is normally quite easy to spot. A real bezel pearl sits embedded in the insert, barely protruding from the surface. It also glows in the dark when exposed to light. Replica pearls sit on top of the bezel and are not luminescent.

Q: What is an "Oyster" case?

A: Rolex coined the term "Oyster" to refer to their water resistant cases. Since the late 50's, Rolex has made watches that are able to be immersed in water and continue to function. This is done by use of gaskets and the "screw-down crown" that seals the movement from moisture. Rolex will mark such watches as "Oyster" on the dial. Rolex does make non-Oyster models, such as early Daytonas. They have standard pushers instead of the later screw-down pushers used in modern models.

Other Brand Questions

Q: The bezel nuts on my Audemars Piguet Royal Oak are yellow gold colored. Is this right?

A: No, all Royal Oaks use white gold bezel nuts and screws. They look "yellow" because of the photographic technology used to take pictures of these watches (improperly adjusted white balance). Because of this, replica makers have assumed they were yellow gold! Unfortunately this is one of the easiest ways to pick out an AP Royal Oak replica from an original.

Spotter's Guide

The following section is a guide to aid in the detection of replica watches. It's not meant as a detailed and definitive review of each individual genuine watch; that would take volumes to do. Instead it's designed to be a resource to quickly identify an individual watch as a suspected replica.

How to Use This Section

Each watch manufacturer has a summary page that describes general information on the replicas made of its models. This includes some information about the brand itself and the vulnerabilities it has to replicas in general. Since this guide does not cover every particular model a manufacturer makes (look for additional models added in the next edition!) there are some comparison photographs and descriptions that highlight other models not covered in detail.

Remember, this guide is designed to cover flaws that you can spot quickly and without opening the watch. So this means covering detailed information on movements and variations within models is not included. Also, the watch band or strap can be (and often is) changed on watches. This means a cheap replica may have a $100 crocodile band fitted to it while a genuine Rolex may be fitted with a cheap NATO strap. This is the easiest thing about a watch to adjust for taste. Many watch owners have a variety of straps to put on a watch depending on their mood.

Audemars Piguet

www.audemarspiguet.com

Jules Audemars

Metropolis

Royal Oak

Audemars Piguet (AP) is vulnerable to a number of replicas of their product line. Most notably, their Royal Oak line has been copied extensively. The quality of the materials is always suspect in Audemars Piguet replicas. The metal bands tend to be rough and difficult to form around the wrist. Also there are a number of Royal Oak replicas made with both "white gold" bezel hex nuts as well as "yellow gold" ones, since the nuts appear to be made of yellow gold in most photographs.

A number of AP models have exhibition backs to show off their highly detailed movements. Many of the counterfeit watches also have exhibition backs, but the movement they reveal is much more primitive. Most replica movements have a gold-tone appearance to them, while the original AP movements are usually highly polished stainless steel.

Quartz movements are also used quite often in replica APs, especially in chronograph models of the Royal Oak. They can typically be identified by the "ticking" of the second hand and the mislabeling of the sub-dials. AP does not have any quartz watches in it's current production line-up.

Models that are copied the most include: Royal Oak (various models), Royal Oak Offshore, Jules Audemars, and Millenary.

Audemars Piguet Link

http://www.network54.com/Forum/200844

A great resource hosted by the people at The PuristS. Plenty of photographs, reviews, and articles on various Audemars Piguet watches.

Jules Audemars Tourbillon

The replica of this watch has the classic exposed bridge that is designed to emulate a tourbillon. On close examination the difference is obvious. Also note the lower quality materials and misplaced elements (such as the date). It bears only a passing resemblance to the original.

Millenary Chronograph

Mislabeled sub-dials and hour markers make this an easy replica to spot. Note that the replica has fused links and a lower quality band.

Pictures courtey of KJM

City of Sails Royal Oak

Indicative of the quartz-based chronograph replicas, the replica of this watch lacks the build quality of the original. The quartz movement and sub-dial spacing gives this counterfeit example away.

Jules Audemars

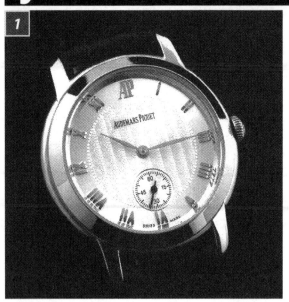

The most obvious flaw is the incorrectly placed second sub-dial.

[2] A close up on the sub-dial.
[3] This replica has the correct crown with the Audemars logo.

The replica is offered in rose gold as well.

Spotter's Tips

Examine the case back if you can. If you view a gold-tone movement through the case back it's likely a counterfeit.

Sub-dial placement is too low on most replicas.

With all Audemars, examine the build quality. A genuine example will be sharp and without flaws, if new.

This model is available in white and yellow gold. Most replica examples have incorrect case back engraving.

There are replicas of this watch based on the ETA 7003 movement that are more accurate than older counterfeits. They even have the sub-dial in the correct location. Look for the incorrect movement in the display back [8].

DANGER Most Dangerous

There are very good ETA-based examples such as the one profiled in these pictures. The case back and the sub dial position are the best clues when performing an examination.

Variants

Replicas of this watch come in stainless steel (passing as white gold), yellow-, and rose-gold plated. Audemars Piguet does not make this watch in rose gold or stainless steel. Replica dials have been seen in white, rose gold, and black.

Varying levels of quality can be found. Poorer examples are easy to spot because of lower quality crystals (made of glass instead of artificial sapphire).

FLASH: Just recently new ETA examples with properly positioned sub-dials have been seen. Beware! These are usually notable for their diamond bezel.

Jules Audemars Major Counterfeit Flaws

Genuine	*Counterfeit*	

Flaw Description

Sub-dial placement
The seconds sub-dial is slightly higher on the dial than the genuine watch.

Case Back
The counterfeit movement in this example is an ETA movement with some embellishments. Note that the replica has applique markings instead of engraving on the movement.

Dial Printing
Examine the dial printing with a loupe. The replica dial printing tends to be less sharp and defined than the genuine watch. Look for deep defined texture to the dial surface.

Genuine Example

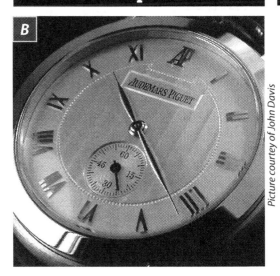

Picture courtesy of John Davis

Other Counterfeit Flaws

- The replica has a laser-etched logo on the buckle, while the genuine example has true engraving.

- The hands on the genuine watch are solid gold and are polished. The replicas tend to use matte hands, typically gold-plated like the case. Look for signs of plating (irregular surface, for example) when examining the watch.

- Genuine case backs will have hallmarks that indicate the case is solid gold. The case back engraving includes the name "Jules Audemars" deeply cut along the flat of the back. [7]

Reference Link

http://www.thepurists.com/watch/features/8ohms/3090/

John Davis has written an excellent article reviewing this watch in detail. His pictures are used here with his permission.

AUDEMARS PIGUET

Jules Audemars

Picture courtesy of John Davis

An excellent photo of a genuine Jules Audemars by John. The watch exudes craftsmanship.

This replica clearly displays the improperly positioned sub-dial. The position of the Audemars logo is also lower than on the original.

Here's the new AP Jules replica, with the sub-dial located in the correct position. Note the incorrect onion crown and the "AUDEMARS PIGUET" on the dial positioned too low. Still, this is a dangerous replica unless you look closely or examine the back.

This replica uses an ETA manual wind movement.

Jules Audemars

A shot of the case back on a genuine Jules Audemars. Note the gilt engraving and the detailed movement.

Picture courtesy of John Davis

This surprisingly close replica uses an ETA movement. One must focus on the details of the case back engraving and the movement. Also note the incorrect onion crown.

This replica uses an incorrect automatic movement instead of the manual that the genuine watch uses. Note also the laser etched logo on the buckle. Laser etching is usually the sign of a replica.

AUDEMARS PIGUET

Metropolis

While similar in appearance, there are significant differences between the replica an genuine on closer inspection.

[2] Note the incorrect laser etching.
[3] This replica's crystal is too thick; it distorts the light.

This replica uses an automatic movement, which i s incorrect for this model. Note the unfinished movement and discolorations on the back.

Spotter's Tips

This Audemars complication is copied with a Japanese movement of surprising accuracy. With the exception of the missing leap year hand and the backwards World Time dial, the watch is functionally identical to the original.

Several flaws stand out, such as the above mentioned missing leap year hand at the 12 o'clock sub-dial. Also, the World Time dial is labeled backwards, so rotating it causes the hour wheel to go in the wrong direction.

Case back and buckle markings are laser engraved instead of cut into the metal. This is easy to spot because there are no grooves to indicate depth for any of the markings.

Some examples have very odd hour markers; the 8, 4, 2, and 10 are exaggerated (more than normal).

The gold plating on this watch discolors easily with use. Look for discolorations and pitting on the case back.

DANGER Most Dangerous

[1] Is an example of the most accurate replica. It's based on a Japanese movement which is visibly incorrect through the exhibition back [4].

Variants

This watch's replicas have been spotted with black, blue, and white dials. Quality varies heavily; most variation takes place in the dial layout.

Audemars does not make this watch in yellow gold; it's available in rose gold and white gold. Replicas are known in stainless steel and yellow gold plate.

Metropolis Major Counterfeit Flaws

| *Genuine* | *Counterfeit* | **Flaw Description** |

Case Back
As with most replicas, the exhibition back reveals the watch has the wrong movement. The simple Japanese movement in the clone is surprisingly flexible, but no match for the genuine in-house movement that Audermars uses.

Dial Flaws
Flaws here include the missing leap year hand and 12 o'clock, and the backward hour track on the World Time dial. Print quality on the replica is good; but examine closely the hour markers. Note the metal pivot on the sub-dial hands used on the genuine watch.

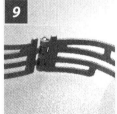 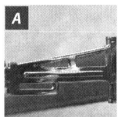

Poor Materials and Markings
This example replica had horrible flash on the deployant that was simply gold plated over. The clasp itself and the case back have laser etching instead of engraving as the genuine has.

Comparison Photographs

Other Counterfeit Flaws

* The lugs on the replica are thicker than the original.

* The genuine watch is much thinner than the replica, mainly because the movement does not have a rotor.

* The genuine watch is manual wind while the replicas are automatic. This is easily distinguishable by the rotor on the counterfeit watch.

Final Look
This watch was not made in yellow gold, as is this replica. Always look for two hands at the 12 o'clock sub-dial. Replicas drop the leap year hand, leaving simply the month indicator.

AUDEMARS PIGUET

Royal Oak

Note the yellow bezel screws and the incorrect dial functions.

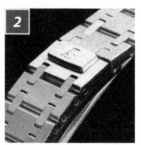

[2] While this band has the correct clasp design, [3] as does this one, both have laser etching, which is the sign of a replica.

This replica has a good dial and the correct white gold screws.

Spotter's Tips

There are a variety of Royal Oak models on the market, both replica and genuine. Most of the high-end replicas are fairly accurate, being based on an ETA movement.

For some reason there are a lot of replica watches of the "Fondation" edition of the Royal Oak. This watch was a limited production model, yet a great number of replicas are based on this watch. It's notable by the embossed tree pattern on the dial.

The genuine watch is available in quartz and automatic. NONE of the genuine chronographs are quartz-based, while all of the replica chronographs use a quartz movement. You can tell if the movement is quartz by the "ticking" movement of the second hand.

Band quality is typically quite poor on replicas; the bands tend to be stiff and inflexible. The general finish of the watch look rough compared to an original.

One big flaw on replicas is the use of gold-tone bezel screws instead of white gold screws.

DANGER Most Dangerous

ETA-based models with correct case screws (white gold versus yellow) are fairly accurate. If the watch has a display back, examine the movement. Audemars has highly decorated movements, while the replicas may have a only a decorated rotor and a gold tone.

Variants

There are many variants to this watch: automatic, quartz, chronograph, metal band, rubber strap, etc. The best advice is to focus on obvious flaws, such as the gold-tone bezel screws, display back, and the quality of the band. These are universal across most of the model line.

Also, if the watch has an embossed tree on the dial it may be counterfeit. This is a common dial pattern on many replicas of this watch.

Richard Brown

Royal Oak Major Counterfeit Flaws

Genuine	Counterfeit	**Flaw Description**

Bezel Nuts
Because they photograph a shade of yellow, many replica makers use gold-tone screws in their bezels. This is incorrect; the genuine watch uses white gold screws to contrast the stainless steel case and bezel.

Case Back
Most Royal Oaks have a solid case back. Many replicas use a display or exhibition case back, which usually displays a pretty plain ETA movement. Sometimes they'll dress up the rotor with Audemars logos, but for the most part the movement is unmodified. When Audemars does use a display back the movement is decorated.

 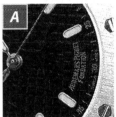

Dial Detail
Look for "Fondation" on the dial, or an embossed tree. This usually points to a replica. The degree of detail to the dial on most replicas is poor; the genuine Royal Oak has a sharp and defined dial pattern.

Genuine Example

Other Counterfeit Flaws

- Chronograph versions of this watch are automatic, not quartz.

- Read carefully the case back. Some Royal Oak replicas are notorious for their spelling errors; things like "NIMITED EDITION" and "MADE IN SWISS."

Reference Link

http://www.timezone.com/library/horologium/horologium631670172488072079

An excellent article on the construction of a Royal Oak. Great pictures for comparison.

AUDEMARS PIGUET

Breitling

Spotter's Tips

Breitling, as a manufacturer, makes high-quality timepieces to extraordinary standards. Their watches are held to a tight level of quality control and construction, and their movements are submitted to COSC for certification.

Most Breitling replicas no where near live up to the level of quality of the original. They are typically based on quartz movements, while most Breitling originals are based on variants of modified ETA movements. Look closely at the watch second hand for "ticking" associated with quartz movements.

All current Breitling models are equipped with an anti-reflective coating on the crystal. If the watch you are examining offers reflections when viewing the watch in normal lighting conditions it may be a replica. Most replicas use a mineral glass crystal which has a slight greenish tint to it and scratches quite easily. Breitling uses a non-scratch sapphire crystal on all of its current models.

Breitling has a small security device on all of their watches made since 1999. Between the 11 and 12 o'clock position on the outside edge of the bezel is a small engraved Breitling logo.

Breitling Link
http://www.irming.com/bfaq/
The Unofficial Breitling FAQ - An excellent source of information on the Breitling brand. It's associated with the Breitling forum on Timezone.

Bentley Chronograph

A popular model this year, this watch is heavily counterfeited with many making their way to eBay auctions. Be very cautious about buying this watch in the secondary market. The replicas are usually pretty easy to spot, check the sub-dials and the bezel. Also, the metal used in the genuine watch is typical of Breitling: it looks like it was carved from a single piece of steel. Replicas have never emulated this quality of construction.

Breitling Chrono Avenger

A genuine Breitling bezel is carefully cut and sharply defined. Most replicas use a stamped bezel that shows deformity in the grooves. As with most replica chronographs, this example has a quartz movement.

Chronomat

There are some Valjoux 7750-based replicas of this watch on the market which emulates the sub-dial functions correctly. As usual, the quality of the steel, the bezel grooves, and the missing anti-reflective coating give away this replica.

Montbrillant Datora

Here's an example of a copy that tries real hard, yet still misses the mark by a mile. Missing complications (day and month), misplaced sub-dials, and poor quality materials (typically chromed brass) give this one away at first glance.

Emergency Mission

Silver sub-dials and quartz movements are a good sign of a replica with Breitling. This example shows the typically bad bezel and poor materials. Always check the back of a Breitling for proper model and serial numbers.

Cartier

www.cartier.com

Roadster

Divan

Tank Francaise

The Cartier brand has proven to be very vulnerable to counterfeiting. I believe this is mainly because Cartier uses quartz movements extensively (which are easy for counterfeiters to replicate) and because of the simplicity of design in many of their models.

Spotting a replica Cartier involves observation and common sense. A $2,500 watch should not have a cheap, flimsy band. They shouldn't have fuzzy dials or balky crowns.

One of the most common flaws that replica Cartiers exhibit are incorrectly colored hands. Cartier uses blued-steel hands on many of their white-dialed models, while using rhodium-plated hands on their dark face watches.

Most replica manufacturers use a blue enamel to simulate the blued-steel hands that is much to bright. The difference is apparent when comparing the two. If the hands appear bright blue (almost an electric blue) they are probably enameled.

Models that seem most vulnerable to better quality counterfeits are: Roadster, Divan, Tank Francaise, and Santos.

Cartier Link
http://forums.timezone.com/index.php?t=threadt&frm_id=17
Timezone has a vibrant Cartier following. Stop in and listen, or ask questions of the resident experts.

Tortue

A very expensive watch, this model has several clones with different variations. This example is fairly accurate from the front, but the exhibition case back shows a Japanese manual movement. Look for misprints such as "eighteem jewels" on the movement, indicating a replica.

Tank a vis

This replica is made from a cheap chrome-plated brass or pot metal. Also note the poor function displays and the incorrect hands. The quality of materials and finish show up this counterfeit.

Santos PM

An example of a two-tone Santos, this replica is fairly close to the original. Examine the hands (look for bright blue hands on the replica) and the "Cartier" in the 7 hour marker. Dial quality is also key to spotting Cartier replicas.

Pasha Chronograph

The Pasha is a frequently copied model, yet few can match the quality of the original. Note the difference in quality of bezel, dial, and sub-dials.

Divan

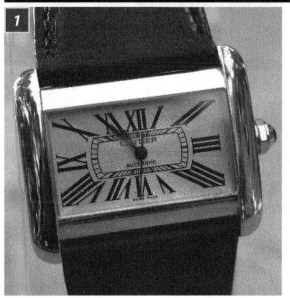

This replica is visually close to the genuine. The blue hands are not as evident in this photo.

[2] Note the dial texture and the "Cartier" in the "VII."
[3] ETA movement used in a Divan replica.

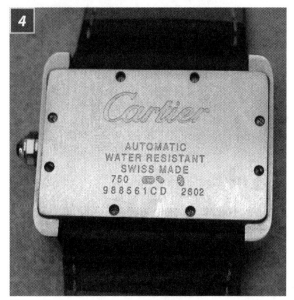

This replica has an accurate case back, but is given away by the rose gold metal.

Spotter's Tips

There are several different counterfeit examples of the Cartier Divan on the market. They range from poor quality quartz models (with mislabeled case backs) to high-end ETA-based examples that are very difficult to spot.

Overall, the best method of identification is to look at certain key aspects: The crown gem, guilloche dial, and the hands. Enameled bright blue hands are the sign of a counterfeit. So is a rose gold case.

If you get to handle the watch or ask for photographs examine the back of the case. It should be secured with 8 small screws. Also, there should be two small screws on either side of the case.

DANGER Most Dangerous

A stainless steel ETA-based example is the most dangerous replica seen to date of this model. It avoids many of the flaws of most counterfeit watches, yet retains the blue hands and the cheap-looking cabochon (gem) on the crown.

Variants

This watch has replicas in stainless steel, rose gold, and yellow gold. The genuine watch does not come in rose gold.

The genuine watch comes in automatic, quartz, and ladies versions. Beware quartz watches labeled automatic. The are examples of this watch with diamonds embedded in the case. The replica versions of this model are fairly easy to spot by the poorly set diamonds and the overall poor quality of the design.

Divan Major Counterfeit Flaws

Genuine	Counterfeit	Flaw Description

Hands
Replica hands are bright blue instead of "blued" (chemically treated and then heated to give a "gun metal" type bluish sheen).

Case Back
The case back should have 8 screws attaching the case back. Some lower quality replicas only have 4 screws securing the case back.

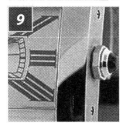 

Crown Jewel
The jewel on the crown of the replica is simply blue tinted glass or crystal. On the genuine watch it's a faceted sapphire, which has a deep lustrous blue color.

Comparison Photographs

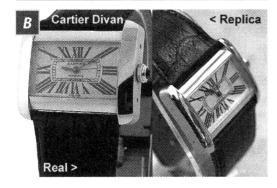

Other Counterfeit Flaws

♦ The back should have engraved "Cartier" not "Roadster" as on some poorer counterfeits.

♦ On gold models look at the sharpness of the engraving on the case back. Plated counterfeits have a slightly rounded appearance to the engraving, instead of sharp as an original.

♦ Dial should have a silver guilloche (textured) appearance.

♦ The Roman "VII" should have one leg of the "V" spell out "Cartier". Some counterfeits mistakenly use the "X" instead.

♦ There is no genuine rose gold model. The real Divan comes in stainless steel or yellow gold. There are versions that have the case studded with diamonds, but they are exceedingly expensive.

CARTIER

Divan

Make sure if the watch is an automatic (smooth, sweeping movement of the second hand, not ticking) that it's labeled "Automatic" on the dial. Genuine quartz versions of this watch exist without this label.

The case back on this replica is very accurate. If it wasn't rose gold (which Cartier does not produce a watch in this color) then it would be difficult to pick out as counterfeit.

Still, the case has a plated look to it. The engraving is a bit blunted, as if it was plated over.

The blue hands on this replica are easy to spot in most lighting conditions. Sometimes they appear black if not illuminated properly.

Divan

A close up of the dial of a replica Divan. This example has the correct dial pattern. Some replicas have a plain dial; look also for the word "Cartier" embedded in the 7 o'clock numeral.

This is a close-up shot of a replica crown gem. Note how glassy and "washed out" it appears. Genuine crown gems are dark and have depth to the surface.

This replica has the correct side case screws. Some replicas use overly large screws on the sides.

The Divan is a bold watch, pointing Cartier in a new direction. Armed with the knowledge in this book you'll be able to spot a genuine one from a replica.

This photo shows a replica with it's blue hands, poor cabochon, and rose gold case.

CARTIER

Roadster

Incorrect blue hands give this replica away.

 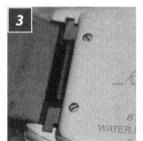

[2] Close-up on Dial, [3] Quick Release end link.

Blue hands, white date wheel and non-factory strap give this watch away as counterfeit.

Spotter's Tips

The Roadster is heavily counterfeited because of its popularity. Most examples are fairly easy to spot if you are observant.

Major flaws include center hour track markers at the 3 o'clock position (under the cyclops). Incorrect blue hands on dark faced models are also common.

On Arabic numeral dials the "SWISS MADE" should line up with the bottom of the "6" indicator.

Genuine dark-faced Roadsters have black date wheels with white numerals. Light-faced watches are the exact opposite.

This watch has a quick release bracelet that is attached with special clips between the lugs. If the watch has a normal spring bars (especially on a leather band) it's a counterfeit.

Another big flaw is the date wheel size. The numerals should fill the date window. They are actually angled to fit because of the trapezoidal shape of the date window.

DANGER Most Dangerous

There are some very accurate ETA-based examples of this watch as replicas. They have great dial quality, but may slip up by printing minute markers under the cyclops. They still have the incorrectly sized date wheel (it will not fill the window).

Variants

This watch has several dial variations as well as being available in yellow gold. A vast majority of the replicas with black dials will have incorrect blue hands.

There is a chronograph version of this watch that also is heavily counterfeited. The genuine watch is larger than the base Roadster. It's also automatic as opposed to the quartz replicas of this model. As always, read dial printing closely for quality of print and accuracy of markings.

Roadster Major Counterfeit Flaws

Genuine	Counterfeit	**Flaw Description**

Hands/Dial Combination
Blue hands on a dark-faced watch are incorrect. Dark dials should have stainless steel (actually rhodium plate) hands. Some of the higher-end counterfeits do correct this.

Dial Printing
Some otherwise accurate replicas get wrong the dial printing; the quality of the print is fuzzy and inconsistent.

Date Wheel
On dark dialed watches the date wheel should have a black background and white numerals. Light colored dials should have the normal white background with black numerals. Most, but not all, replicas get this wrong.

Comparison Photographs

Cartier Roadster

<Real Repl.>

Other Counterfeit Flaws

- Enameled blue hands are common on replicas.

- The "Swiss Made" should line up with the bottom of the "6" on the dial.

- Always check luminosity of the dial. A genuine model should have brightly glowing hands when exposure to light.

- There should be no holes in the side of the case for spring bars.

- The band should have screws instead of pins and be of a substantial weight. A larger screw should connect the special clip end piece to the band.

- The case back should have "Roadster" deeply engraved in the center, and the legend Roadster should be larger than the Cartier engraving. If it's not, the watch is probably a replica.

- There should be 8 screws attaching the case back to the watch. Some cheaper examples have engraved "screw heads" to simulate this.

- The dial should have two layers to it, with a depth to the center of the dial.

- The hour hand should stay within the margins of the inner ring of the dial.

CARTIER

Roadster

Here we have two different Roadster replicas, each with it's own flaws. The watch on the left has the proper hour marker size (the numeral "6" lines up with "Swiss Made" properly) yet misses the mark by having the inner minute track on the dial extend below the cyclops.

The watch on the right gets the minute track right but the numerals on the dial are too small.

Both watches have an incorrect date font; it does not angle to fit the window.

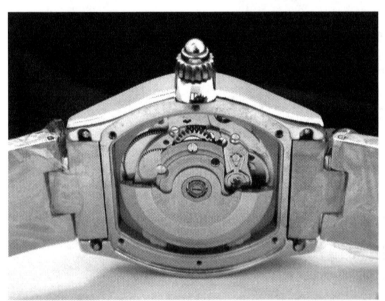

Here the case back has been removed from a replica to display the gold-toned ETA movement used to power it.

The movement is held in place with a white plastic spacer and has no Cartier logo or markings.

Note this watch uses the incorrect end links. It uses spring bars instead of the quick release system that the original uses.

This replica has several glaring problems. First of all, the dark blue hands with the dark dial is incorrect. This would make it difficult to tell the time in poor lighting conditions.

Secondly, the date wheel has a white background with black numerals. The genuine watch has just the opposite: black background and white numerals.

Lastly, the band is incorrect; it attaches with spring pins instead of the special quick release attachments the original uses.

Roadster

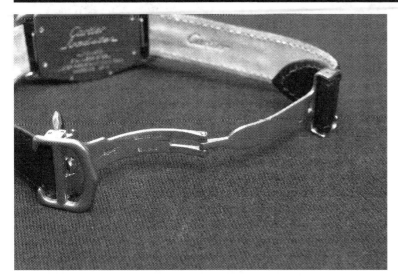

Up until recently there hasn't been a strap for Roadster replicas with the correct quick release attachment. This example is fairly accurate yet uses a cheaply finished deployant. The stamping and quality of materials is substandard to Cartier's level of manufacture.

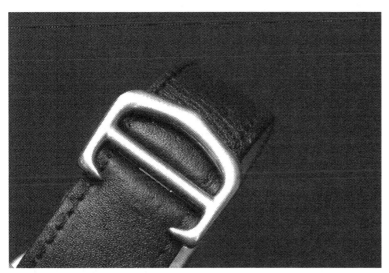

Notice the poor quality of the metal on this replica deployant. Cartier uses a higher grade of polished steel that doesn't have the "grainy" appearance that this clasp displays.

Detail on a replica strap; notice the quick release connector to the case. This is correct compared to spring bars used on some replicas.

CARTIER

Tank Francaise

The bright blue hands on this watch mark it as a replica.

[2] Replica makers have successfully duplicated the clasp.
[3] Note the counterfeit clasp in the folded position.

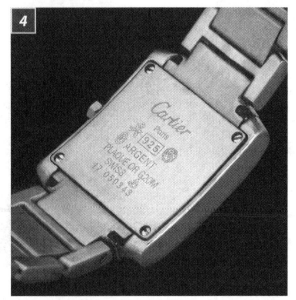

This watch is stainless steel, yet has the hallmarks of a solid gold model. This is a common practice amongst counterfeiters.

Spotter's Tips

Tank Francaise is available in a number of different variations and two different sizes: small, powered by a quartz movement, and large, using an automatic movement.

When evaluating a Cartier Tank, first look at the hands. If they look bright blue instead of dark blue or black, then the watch is probably a replica. Most Cartier replicas use enameled hands instead of the blued or blackened steel that Cartier uses in their watches.

Also, examine the case back. Many Cartier replicas are available in gold, two-toned, or stainless steel. In order to save money, the replica makers use the same case back, no matter what material the watch is made out of. This means that if you see gold hallmarks on a stainless steel watch (such as in [4]), you are probably dealing with a replica.

DANGER Most Dangerous

Some Tank replicas actually use the same movement as the original (based on the ubiquitous ETA), down to the Cartier logo on the rotor. Always examine the hands when looking at any Cartier.

Variants

This watch is available in small size (women's) and large size (men's), in yellow and white gold, as well as stainless steel and two-toned yellow gold/stainless.

Replicas are known of all examples. The gold plating tends to be poor; always check for gold hallmarks on the case back.

Tank Francaise Major Counterfeit Flaws

| *Genuine* | *Counterfeit* | **Flaw Description** |

Enameled Blue Hands
A common flaw with most Cartier replicas, bright blue enameled hands are common on this model. They differ from the genuine watch's blued-steel hands.

Crown Gem
The size and shape of the crown varies on replicas of this model. They use a lighter crystal instead of the rich, dark sapphire that is used on the genuine watch.

Case Back
The replica manufacturers use the same case whether it's destined to be for a gold plated model or a stainless steel example. In [A] you can see the gold hallmarks and "ARGENT" markings which are used on solid gold models. This is a common mistake on replicas of watches that are available in gold and stainless steel.

Comparison Photographs

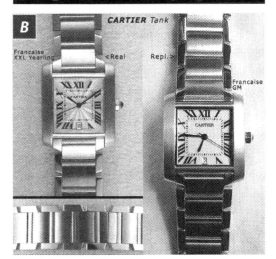

Other Counterfeit Flaws

- The size and shape of the hands is known to be off on most replicas. Examine the photos on Cartier's web site, or better yet, visit your local dealer to get a closer look at the original.

- The print quality of the dial is very important on a Cartier. If the dial looks fuzzy, or the markers indistinct, then it probably is a replica.

- Look for the name "Cartier" spelled out on the leg of the "VII" on the dial. If it's missing, or located on another numeral, it's a sign of a counterfeit watch.

- Cartier does not use laser etching. Many replicas have etching instead of the proper engraving.

CARTIER

Omega

www.omega.ch

Seamaster Professional

Speedmaster "Replica"

Seamaster 007

Speedmaster Broad Arrow

Omega has been subjected to some of the most accurate counterfeit watches on the market. There is a large secondary market for Omega parts which the counterfeiters tap into when making their clones.

The best examples are Seamasters and Speedmasters, these are copied even to the degree of using the same movement that the genuine model uses, albeit without the finishing and adjusting that Omega watches go through.

Omega Seamasters are the most commonly copied, and potentially some of the accurate replicas on the market at the high end. These examples are based on ETA movements with good quality stainless steel cases.

The bands on these tend to be of a varying quality; watch for corrosion on the inside of links. This are a problem for many Omega counterfeits. Look for fused links and cheap materials. An Omega metal band is a solid piece of engineering.

Omega Links
http://www.chronocentric.com/galleries/rogues_intro.shtml
Chronocentric's awesome site on counterfeit Omegas. It's an in-depth examination of spotting replicas and a great source of Omega knowledge in general. Highly recommended.
http://home.xnet.com/~cmaddox/moonwatch_casebacks.html
A great resource for shots of case backs for Speedmaster Professional "Moon watches" and their variants.

Deville Chronograph

The replicas of this watch are typically of low quality. Notice the difference in the hands and the dial printing. The genuine watch is highly polished and finished, while the replica is made of poor quality stainless steel or worse, plated brass or pot metal.

Speedmaster Day-Date

At first glance, some replicas of this watch are quite credible. But after a detailed analysis the differences are quite easy to spot.

Replica build quality is typically poor. Note the difference in sub-dials and the date window on the replica. The genuine watch uses a forth hand to indicate the date on the inner ring. Also, the genuine has day and month indicated at 12 o'clock.

Museum

This is an example of the replica manufacturers probably never actually seeing the watch in question. While in spirit the watches are similar, the counterfeiters added features and functions that don't exist on the genuine watch.

Seamaster Professional

[1] The Seamaster replica is one of the most accurate on the market.

[2] Notice the quality of the materials in the clasp.
[3] Higher-end replicas use ETA movements labeled as Omegas.

[4] This model is also available with a blue dial and different bezel.

Spotter's Tips

There are some VERY accurate replicas of the Seamaster Pro floating around. They are accurate down to the anti-magnetic shield over the movement, and are made of a high grade of stainless steel. They have the same weight and a decent build quality.

Replicas of this watch have a crystal that's a bit too thick and without the anti-reflective coating. Also, the dial printing can be inaccurate, using the printing from the mid-sized model instead of the full-sized. Fortunately high-quality replicas are not as common as poorer examples.

Lower-end counterfeits have horrible build quality and some creative interpretations of the genuine watch (strange dial colors, incorrect hands, etc.). These usually can be picked out by the poor quality and the lightness of the watch.

DANGER Most Dangerous

High-end ETA replicas are very accurate when compared to the original. They have accurate markings and a heavy band. Flaws to look for include the anti-reflective coating on the crystal and fused links on the band.

Variants

This watch comes with blue and black faces. The black face comes with a black background date wheel with white numerals. The blue faced watch comes with a engraved bezel as well as the stamped insert bezel that the black example comes with.

The blue dial watch comes with a white background date wheel with black numerals.

Seamaster Professional Major Counterfeit Flaws

| *Genuine* | *Counterfeit* | **Flaw Description** |

Seamaster Script
On full-size models the "Seamaster" script should be the same size as the rest of the print on the dial. Many replicas instead use the printing from the mid-sized watch which has the "Seamaster" in larger print. Replicas are of the full-size model.

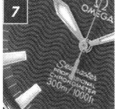 

Dial Pattern Quality
The dial should have depth and texture to it. Some cheaper replicas simply use a printed dial which looks flat. You can see this depth by examining the dial while viewing the watch at different angles.

Anti-Reflective Coating
Genuine Seamasters have an AR coating that reduces reflectivity. No replica will have this coating; replica crystals also tend to "coke bottle" when viewed at an extreme angle and will show normal reflections.

Comparison Photographs

Other Counterfeit Flaws

- The luminosity of the dial is a good give-away for this model. Replicas typically will have decent luminosity on the hands, but the dial will not glow or will glow poorly.

- The band on many poorly made counterfeits will have fused segments to the links instead of a "layered" band which has links made up of several parts. Corrosion is also a big problem on counterfeit bands.

- Just as a note: Omega uses pins in their bands, so the normal warning about screws does not apply to this manufacturer.

- The gas release valve at 10 o'clock is non-functional on replicas.

Seamaster GMT
Here is an example of the quality of certain Omega replicas. This counterfeit watch is a GMT version of the Seamaster. Notice how sharp the dial and bezel are; but most importantly, notice the quality of the luminescence from the hour markers and hands.

OMEGA

Seamaster Professional

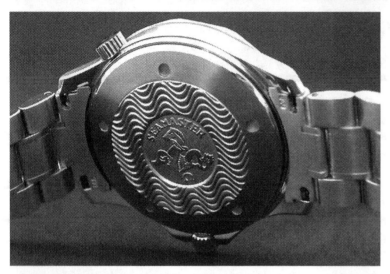

This is a photograph of a replica case back. This high-end replica has the correct markings and engraving.

Notice the "Seamaster" in the center. Many low-end replicas will have an incorrect case back, without these markings.

Here is the extent that some replicas will go to; this counterfeit Seamaster has an anti-magnetic shield over the movement.

The same replica has "OMEGA" engraved on the movement's rotor. This makes this counterfeit more difficult to tell from the genuine watch. Note that this level of detail doesn't extend to all Omega replicas, just to the high-end models.

Most Omega replicas are made of poor materials and are fairly easy to spot. It's replicas of this higher quality that are the most dangerous.

Seamaster Professional

Here is the case back interior of the Omega replica.

Note the flaw on this replica dial. The word "Seamaster" should be the same size as the rest of the text on the dial. This style of print actually emulates the print on a mid-sized Seamaster.

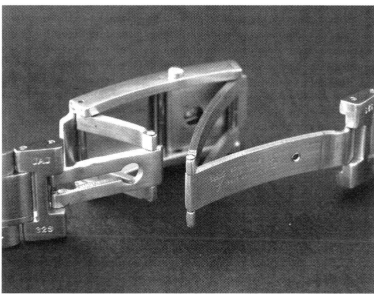

Note the detail on this high-end replica clasp, including stamps and markings. The clasp and band are made of high grade stainless steel. The weight and feel is very similar to a genuine Seamaster.

OMEGA

Seamaster Professional 007

Note the poor dial and incorrect (Rolex-style) date wheel.

[2] This watch has a fused-band style bracelet.
[3] This case back should have "007" embossed in the center.

Notice the glare on the crystal and the flat "007" on the dial.

Spotter's Tips

This watch's replicas are made in a variety of build qualities. These vary from very cheap and easy to spot, to the more difficult high-end ETA models that use OEM-quality cases, bands, and improved dials.

The dial on this model is a typically the weak point in replicas. They will use a flat dial with a printed texture as opposed to the richly detailed dial that the genuine watch uses. Note the flawed dial in [1] compared to the detail in [5].

The case and band materials are also an area to inspect. Low end replicas will use a low grade steel or plated pot metal for the case.

Note the raised "007" on the genuine dial [5]. Many replicas will simply have this printed on the dial.

DANGER Most Dangerous

ETA-based examples using OEM-quality cases, bands, and textured dials are the most difficult to spot. They even have the correct markings on the case back.

Variants

This watch is available both with the limited edition "007" dial and a standard Seamaster-style dial for the rest of the model run. Replicas exist for both style of watches.

The watch is available with blue and black dials.

Seamaster Professional 007 Major Counterfeit Flaws

Genuine	*Counterfeit*	**Flaw Description**

Dial Printing
The genuine watch has a texture to the dial face. Many replicas use simply a printed pattern that is missing this feature.

Date Wheel and Window
Note the incorrect date font on the replica [8]. The size of the date window is also smaller than on the genuine [7].

Fused Band
Genuine Seamasters have band links made of multiple parts. Many replicas use a fused band instead, with each link emulating the look of a genuine one. The replica bands tend to be stiffer and can suffer from corrosion problems.

Comparison Photographs

Other Counterfeit Flaws

♦ The quality of the hands on many replicas is quite poor. They are too thick or have luminous material applied incorrectly.

♦ Note the difference in bezels between the watches [B]. The font on the bezel differs greatly between the replica and the genuine watch.

OMEGA

Speedmaster "Replica"

While this replica is put together well, it's not accurate to any Omega model in production.

[2] The clasp on this model is well made-pointing to it possibly being an aftermarket bracelet for real Omegas. [3] Correct replica serial number.

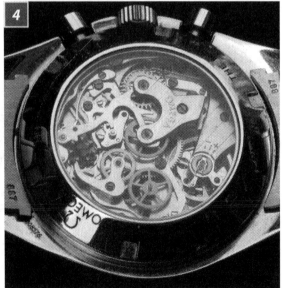

The display case back shows a Lemania movement, yet with "Omega" in applique on the bridge. This applique is really just a sticker; it can easily fall off and get caught in the movement.

Spotter's Tips

This replica watch is an example of the counterfeit manufacturers having no direct knowledge of the products they are duplicating. This particular watch is similar to an Omega Professional, yet has the wrong hands, dial color, bezel, and sub-dial spacing.

The replica uses the hand-wound Lemania 861 movement, which is also used in some Omega chronographs. It's finished quite similarly, yet the replica uses gold-tone appliques on the bridgework to simulate the Omega engraving.

Notice the "Automatic" on the dial, which is incorrect for this watch.

The finish on this watch is quite good, yet it's miles away from the genuine in terms of accuracy.

DANGER Most Dangerous

The Lemania movement-based replica above is the most accurate, yet it has plenty of flaws to pick it out as a replica.

Variants

This watch is available with a black or white dial. It may be seen with a metal band or leather strap; it was available both ways from the factory.

Speedmaster "Replica" Major Counterfeit Flaws

| *Genuine* | *Counterfeit* | **Flaw Description** |

Dial Printing
The replica's dial is incorrectly labeled as an "Automatic," even though the case back displays a manual wind movement. Look closely at the quality of the printing and condition of the dial; dirt, fingerprints, or even hairs are known on replicas.

Sub-dial Spacing
Note the difference in sub-dial spacing.

 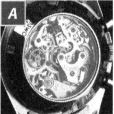

Case Back
The genuine Replica has a solid case back, while the "replica" Replica uses the case back of another model.

Comparison Photographs

Other Counterfeit Flaws

Real   Replica

* Many replicas have flaws in the bezel or case back engraving.

* The replica's movement does not have a functional sub-dial at 6 o'clock. Instead, the hand of the 6 o'clock sub-dial is linked to the hour hand. It will always point in the same direction.

OMEGA

Speedmaster "Replica"

Here is the exhibition window on a replica. Note the gold applique "OMEGA" on the movement. This particular counterfeit movement does not have a functional sub-dial at 6 o'clock.

Note the correct-style serial number stamped on the lug in the lower left corner. The bracelet has stampings on the end link.

None of the engraving on this watch is laser etched, which is a common flaw for some replicas.

This is a higher-end replica, probably using an aftermarket band. Unlike some replicas that have fused links this band has five individual segments per link, like the original.

Detail of the dial print on an Omega replica. On this example the printing is fairly sharp. Note the oxidation and discoloring on the hour markers and hands.

Speedmaster "Replica"

From this photograph it's easy to see how the 6 o'clock sub-dial is linked to the hour hand. Notice how they are pointing in the same direction.

Note the misprinted 1000 in the bezel detail at 2 o'clock. This watch is fitted with a Plexiglas (plastic) crystal.

Even though this particular watch is fitted with a manual movement it's labeled with "Automatic" on the dial. As always be observant and look at each detail independently.

OMEGA

Speedmaster Broad Arrow

Available on either strap or metal band, this replica is very similar to the genuine model.

The bezel [2] and case back [3] on this replica are fairly accurate.

This replica has a high quality strap. Remember, straps can be replaced with one of a better quality by any owner.

Spotter's Tips

The Omega Broad Arrow is a very popular chronograph in the brand's product line. There are several counterfeit watches based on this model in production.

Fortunately the replicas do not have correctly functional sub-dials. As with any chronograph, try the pushers to make sure they work.

On the replicas, the center second hand acts as the main second hand, unlike the genuine who's second hand is at the 9 o'clock sub-dial.

The hands on the replicas are bright blue; painted instead of "blued."

Look closely at the date window at 6 o'clock. On replicas this window is usually too small to view the whole date.

DANGER Most Dangerous

The most accurate version of this watch has a high quality band (with segmented links) and an accurate dial. It's biggest shortcoming is that the sub-dials are non-functional, or function as day/date/24-hour hands.

Variants

This watch has replica examples with white and black dials. White-dialed replicas have very shiny blue hands while the black-faced examples have steel hands.

Most examples show up on bands which are very accurate and quite heavy. Some may have their bands replaced with leather straps of varying quality.

Speedmaster Broad Arrow Major Counterfeit Flaws

Genuine   *Counterfeit*   **Flaw Description**

Date Window Too Small
On this replica example the date window is much smaller than the date wheel font, causing the numbers to be cut off [6].

Non Functional Sub-dials
In order to have the sub-dials positioned properly Broad Arrow replicas use a movement that has sub-dials that function as day/date/24 hour. Always attempt to start the stop watch function to insure the movement functions appropriately.

Hand Color and Dial
As with most replicas emulating blued-steel, the hands may be a bright enamel blue. Note also the differences in the dial printing and hour markers.

Comparison Photographs

Other Counterfeit Flaws

- ◆ Replica Broad Arrows lack the anti-reflective coating of the genuine watch.

- ◆ Check the bezel for errors in printing. This seems to be fairly common in Omega replicas.

- ◆ This watch does not have a display case back.

This genuine Broad Arrow can be destinguished by the size of its date window at 6 o'clock.

OMEGA

Officine Panerai

www.panerai.com

Luminor Marina

Luminor Base

Panerai has been a popular brand with today's superstars, and because of it's popularity its product line has been copied extensively by the counterfeit manufacturers. The brand has a distinctive look and form factor which has been duplicated with some success. The most popular models to copy seem to be the base Panerais, mainly because of the lack of a date window.

The genuine base model is 44mm in diameter while many of the replicas measure only 40mm. Panerais with exhibition backs show a detailed movement. In comparison, the average replica either shows a solid back (with the incorrect "Diver Professional" engraved on the back") or an incorrect gold-tone movement.

Recently several replicas based on the Unitas movement have come onto the market. Panerai uses a modified version of this movement in it's base models. The replica's movement is very close in appearance to Panerai watch, but is not finished to the level of the genuine. We'll show you how to tell the difference.

One of the easiest ways to spot a replica Panerai is to look at the crown. Counterfeit Panerais have penny-thin crowns that don't fill out the crown guard. Even many of the higher-end Unitas-based replicas have too-thin crowns. Also, all current model Panerais have an anti-reflective coating on the crystal that reduces the appearance of reflections. The crystal should "disappear" at certain angles.

For those Panerai's with a date window, dark colored dials have a dark (black or blue) colored background to the date wheel with white numerals. The font is a bold sans-serif (no "tails" to the end of the numbers). No known replicas actually have this correct date wheel.

Panerais typically are sold with a finely made strap or a metal band. The metal band is a work of art; separate interlocking links that has a substantial feel and surgical steel perfection. If the band feels light weight or the links are attached with pins then it's probably a replica.

Panerai Link

http://www.paneristi.com

One of the best brand-specific watch sites on the net. All things Panerai are discussed on this site. They have an excellent research area that documents every model.

General Panerai Details

This is an example of an early Panerai replica. The quality of the watch is poor; it has a crystal that is too thick and a crown that is too thin. Also, the second hand design is incorrect and it moves with a jerky motion.

Notice the date wheel and cyclops. This is incorrect and poorly implemented (round instead of square). Overall, an easy watch to spot as counterfeit.

Another shot of the replica crown. Many lower-end replicas use this penny-thin crown instead of the thicker genuine crown. Note the lack of a "lip" around the edge of the crown.

No genuine Panerais use a crown this thin.

General Panerai Details

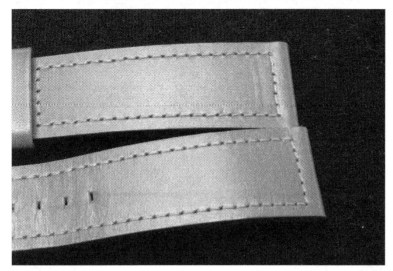

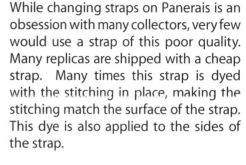

While changing straps on Panerais is an obsession with many collectors, very few would use a strap of this poor quality. Many replicas are shipped with a cheap strap. Many times this strap is dyed with the stitching in place, making the stitching match the surface of the strap. This dye is also applied to the sides of the strap.

The quality of materials is very poor. While straps are usually tough to quantify on a watch, one this poor is typically the sign of a replica.

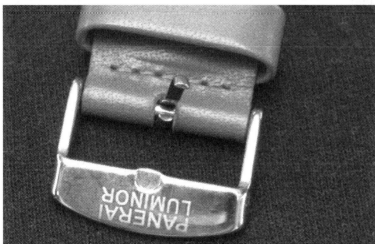

Detail of the replica strap buckle. Notice the laser-etched writing on the buckle. Panerai never uses laser etching on their watches.

The shape of the buckle is incorrect as well. Modern Panerai buckles use a screw to secure the buckle and tang to the strap; this replica uses a spring bar.

PANERAI

Luminor Base

Note the incorrect dial labeling. "MARINA" does not exist on the genuine's dial.

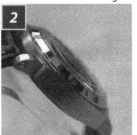

There is a slight green cast to this crystal, typical of mineral glass [2]. The model number and markings on this case back are wrong. [3]

This watch has an ETA movement, and measures only 40mm.

Spotter's Tips

The actual PAM 002 measures 44mm in diameter excluding the crown and guard. Most replicas of this watch measure only 40mm across and look smaller than the genuine watch. Also, there is a difference between the genuine and replica in the lug size: 24mm versus 22mm. Your tape measure will help you determine the actual size.

"DIVER PROFESSIONAL" and other markings on the back of the replicas are usually incorrect.

The dial print should read "LUMINOR" and "PANERAI." Many replicas will be incorrectly labeled "LUMINOR MARINA."

DANGER Most Dangerous

There is a Unitas-based 44mm version with a display back that is very accurate. Look for the incorrect bridges on the movement and the lack of anti-reflective coating.

Variants

In 2002 Panerai changed this model to have a display back. This watch is available in polished and PVD-coated steel, as well as in titanium.

This watch is also available with a white dial as the PAM 112.

Luminor Base Major Counterfeit Flaws

Genuine	Counterfeit	**Flaw Description**

Crown Thickness

One of the biggest flaws in most Panerai replicas is the thickness of the crown. If the crown is as thin or thinner than a quarter the odds are the watch is a replica. Panerai crowns and crown guards are solidly constructed and fit together tightly.

Dial Printing

Note the difference in the dial in this example [8]. "Marina Militare" is incorrect for this model.

Anti-reflective Coating

Modern Panerais have a coating to reduce glare and make the watch easier to read in varying lighting conditions. Replicas lack this coating and the crystal will reflect all light. The genuine crystal seems to disappear in most lighting conditions.

Comparison Photographs

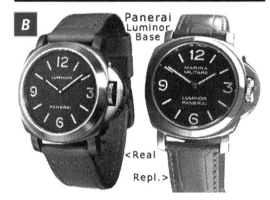

Panerai Luminor Base

< Real

Repl. >

Other Counterfeit Flaws

- The guard lever should close completely and tightly. On many replicas the fit isn't good and the lever sticks up slightly.

PANERAI

Luminor Base

Photo courtesy of Ted

This is an example of the 40mm PAM 002 replica with the incorrect "MARINA MILITARE" dial. Also, note the difference in the "1" in "12" at 12 o'clock.

This particular watch has an aftermarket strap.

In this photograph you can see the greenish tint to the crystal that usually indicates "mineral glass" instead of the correct sapphire crystal. Unless purposefully tinted, a sapphire crystal is colorless.

Photo courtesy of River

This replica of a PAM 114 is very accurate, down to the correct case back design. The biggest flaws on this watch are the missing anti-reflective coating and the incorrect engraving on the movement.

Note also the ill-fitting crown guard lever. It does not fit flush to the case.

Luminor Base

This replica has had the case back removed to display it's ETA movement. Note the plastic spacer between the case and the movement. This is to hold the movement in place so that it doesn't rattle around during use.

This picture shows the display back on a replica of the new PAM 112/114 (which is a later display back version of the PAM 002).

This is an example of the replica with a white dial (PAM 112).

Photo courtesy of River

PANERAI

Luminor Marina

This replica is obviously missing an anti-reflective coating.

[2] Many replicas don't use the screw and tube method that Panerai uses. [3] Note the bad hour markers and second hand.

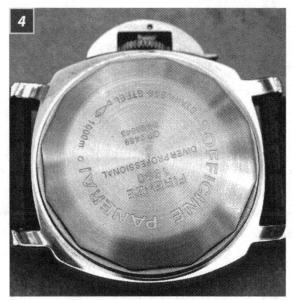

Note the incorrect marking: "DIVER PROFESSIONAL," and the invalid model number.

Spotter's Tips

Panerais are popular watches to counterfeit. Most, fortunately, are of poor quality in terms of materials, and are easily detected.

This particular model has some convincing replicas, until you actually examine them closely. There are enough flaws that you can identify one on the wrist if you look for (mainly the anti-reflective coating, band quality, and the crown size). Once off the wrist it's an easy task to identify most of the other points.

The PAM-001 has a solid case back while the PAM-111 has an exhibition case back. Other than this difference both models are functionally identical. Mid-2004 a replica with an exhibition case back was released that is fairly accurate. Look for an erroneous "TITANIUM" on the case back as a tell.

The solid case back replica has "DIVER PROFESSIONAL" on the back, and often lacks a serial number.

Both of these models should have a 44mm case, not 40mm.

🛑 **DANGER** **Most Dangerous**

The current best replica of this watch is of the PAM-111 model. It has an exhibition case back and decorated movement. The biggest flaw on this watch is the movement's layout and engraving.

Variants

Replicas in 44mm and 40mm are known. They come with a variety of straps with differing levels of quality. As with many Panerai replicas, the factory strap is often replaced with aftermarket ones, so it's not a strong indicator of authenticity.

Some of the replicas have a black-edged second hand, which is uncommon on genuine examples. Most genuine (and many recent replicas) use a white second hand.

No known quality replica metal band for Panerais exist. The poor quality replica bands are easy to spot by their flimsiness and lightweight construction.

t

Luminor Marina Major Counterfeit Flaws

Genuine	Counterfeit

Flaw Description

Case Back
Counterfeit examples have their case back flaws: PAM-001 has incorrectly stamped "Diver Professional", PAM-111 has "TITANIUM" engraved on the back with an exhibition window that is too small. More modern replicas actually accurately duplicate the case back on this model.

Anti-reflective Coating (AR)
All of the modern Panerais have a coating on the crystal that reduces reflections. So far none of the replicas have managed to duplicate this procedure. View the watch at a variety of angles. AR-coated crystals will be invisible at most angles.

Crown Size
Typically, replica crowns are much thinner than their genuine counterparts. The crown at [A] is one-third thinner than a real Panerai, yet there are replica crowns even thinner, approaching the width of a dime or penny.

Comparison Photographs

Real — Replica

Replica crown guard with brushed steel lever.

Other Counterfeit Flaws

- The case should measure 44 mm without the crown guard. There are some 40 mm counterfeit examples. The band should measure 24 mm at the lugs, not 22mm.

- Most genuine Panerais have an all-white second hand. Some older replicas have a black second hand with a white luminous center. Unfortunately, there are variations both in the replicas and genuine models that make this a difficult indicator.

- Replicas have an incorrect or missing model number engraved on the back. Model OP2468 for example is incorrect; the correct model number for the PAM 111 is OP6567.

- The top and bottom markers on the second hand sub-dial should be inset from the "10" and "8" markers on the dial [7]. If they line up with these markers [8] the watch is potentially counterfeit.

- High end PAM-001/111s replicas use a Unitas movement which is very similar to the model that's used in the genuine watch. The main differences are some tweaks Panerai performed, and the quality of the engraving done in order to make it look attractive.

  Try winding the watch; some counterfeiters don't mount the movement correctly, meaning it will move inside the case when you wind it.

- The guard lever should close completely and tightly. On many replicas the fit isn't good and the lever sticks up slightly.

PANERAI

Luminor Marina

A wide shot showing the new Panerai PAM 111 replica. Note the glare on the crystal. This particular watch has been fitted with an aftermarket band. The replica comes with proper tubes and screws that accept a Panerai-style strap.

A shot of the back side of the new Panerai replica. The inset shows an earlier incorrect variation of the replica exhibition case back.

A closer view of the replica movement. It's a Unitas 6497, which is similar to the original Panerai movement. The major flaw here is the difference in the bridge work. Even though this replica appears to be engraved properly there are several differences in the appearance of the back.

Luminor Marina

In an attempt to emulate the anti-reflective coating on a genuine Panerai, this replica manufacturer coated their crystal with a blue film. The film is only visible at certain angles and has the appearance of an AR coating.

Actually it does nothing; it doesn't cut down on glare at all. It just gives the dial a blue cast at certain angles.

An extreme close-up on the movement engraving. Note the screw in the lower right corner. On a true Panerai movement this screw is blue.

While this replica has the appearance of being engraved, in reality it's simply a plate attached to the movement. The layout of the plate is different than the bridgework on a true Panerai.

A genuine PAM 111 movement. The differences are clear when you have the opportunity to compare the two.

Note the differences in the engraving layout and text size. Also, the genuine watch has blue screws and gilt engraving that the replica is missing.

PANERAI

Patek Philippe

www.patek.com

Calatrava 3919

Nautilus

Patek Philippe is one of the best-known high-end watch manufacturers in the world. Unfortunately some of their simpler designs (still costing upwards of US$10,000) have had some credible replicas made in their likeness. The Calatrava line is probably the most vulnerable. The base models have no date wheel and are quite easy to replicate at "Sleeve" level.

Most of the higher-end complication models are not replicated well; the replica watches are too thick, or the build materials are of low quality. Look for exhibition backs that show cheap movements. When Patek uses a display back it shows a beautiful detailed movement. Even the movements hidden behind solid case backs are works of art.

There are several new replicas based on the Poljot. They have two sub-dials and a dial layout similar to a model 5070. This is typical of another segment of Patek replicas: mythical models. Replica manufactures will put the Patek label on a watch that is a copy of another manufacturer's model, or even a totally made up design. As with any watch evaluation, knowledge of the product line, and common sense, are your best tools.

The most accurate Patek Philipe replica is the base Calatrava model. Most of the other current models are replicated in cheap quality examples that are fairly easy to identify.

Patek Philippe Link
http://www.network54.com/Forum/196053
The PuristS web site has an excellent and extensive archive of Patek Philippe information. They also have an active forum and sales/trade area.

Sky Moon

This watch is easily identifiable as a fake by examining the case back. It will show an inexpensive Japanese movement instead of the finely finished Patek movement with a micro rotor.

Also the rotating sidereal dial is only for show on the replica.

World timer

The replica World timer is nearly twice as deep as the genuine watch and is missing a pusher on the left side of the case. The back of the counterfeit watch also shows a cheap movement through the exhibition case back.

The world time inner bezel rotates BACKWARDS on the replica.

Reference 5004

This replica is not even close to the original, although it bears a passing resemblance if you're not familiar with this watch. Note the difference in sub-dial labeling and the missing pushers on the replica.

The gold plating on the replica is also a poor imitation of the original solid gold watch.

Reference 5059

Although similar at first glance there are many differences between the genuine 5059 and the copies. These lie mainly in the quality of the construction and the dimensions of the watch. The replica is nearly twice as thick and the dial quality is sub-par compared to the original.

Note the jump date hands on the genuine are replicated poorly on the replica.

General Patek Philippe

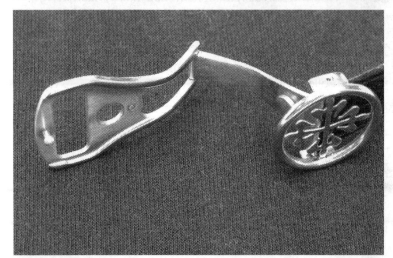

This is a replica clasp off of a counterfeit Patek World Time. Not only is it made of a cheap base metal, it also doesn't work! The craftsmanship is poor and doesn't meet the standards of what you'd expect from a $30,000 watch.

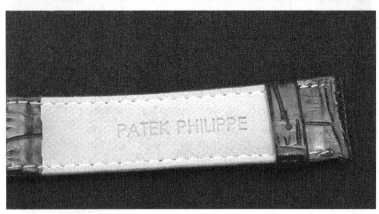

Just because a strap is stamped with a brand name doesn't mean it's original. This replica band has an imitation alligator grain on the surface.

Remember, straps are the easiest thing to change. Unless the owner insists it's original with the watch it may have legitimately been changed to an aftermarket (and possibly poorer quality) strap.

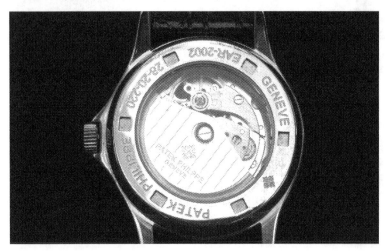

Here is a case back of a Patek World Time replica, showing a poorly finished movement. Note the laser engraving on the movement's rotor and the overall "stamped" appearance to the movement.

Always examine both sides of a watch when doing an evaluation.

PATEK PHILIPPE

Calatrava Ref. 3919

The simple design of the 3919 makes it easy to replicate.

[2] Note the incorrect gold hour markers.
[3] This example has an easy to spot incorrect case back.

The crystal on this replica correctly emulates the original.

Spotter's Tips

The 3919 is vulnerable to counterfeits mainly because of its simplicity. It has no complications and very little inherit detail that need to be copied. Because of this, there are a number of fakes floating around that are fairly credible at first glance.

Always look at the fit and finish of the watch. Genuine Pateks are hand made, and are constructed of some of the finest materials available. Detailed examination will help you identify substandard materials.

Highlights to look for include the domed crystal and sub-dial placement. Also look carefully for the **stamped** gold hallmarks on the case and buckle. Note that Patek uses high quality leather for its straps.

DANGER Most Dangerous

Solid case back replicas in plated gold are potentially the most difficult to identify. Some examples have exhibition backs which show an obviously non-original movement.

Variants

Replicas of the Calatrava come in manual and quartz examples. The quartz movement is typically used in the Calatrava variant that does not have a second hand.

This watch is available in, white, rose, and yellow gold. Replicas are available in each metal color.

Calatrava Ref. 3919 Major Counterfeit Flaws

Genuine	*Counterfeit*	**Flaw Description**

Incorrectly Positioned Sub-dial
The seconds sub-dial should be at least 3 mm away from the "6" marker; almost equidistant to the hub for the main hands. It should not touch or partially cover the "6" marker.

Case Back
If the watch has a display back (gold tone movement typically) it's probably counterfeit. The genuine case will have gold hallmarks.

 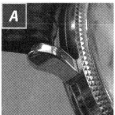

Gold Hallmarks
The genuine 3919 has hallmarks stamped on the sides of the lugs. The replicas don't have any hallmarks at all. They appear as tiny engravings on the side of the lug.

Comparison Photographs

Patek Philippe
Calatrava Ref. 3919

< Real   Repl. >

Picture courtesy of John Davis

johnd@ThePuristS.com

Genuine 3919 Movement

Other Counterfeit Flaws

• The genuine Calatrava has a slightly domed crystal. Be wary of watches with flat crystals. You should see a slight bowing when viewing from the side. Some replicas have this correct crystal.

• Look carefully at the second hand sub-dial markers. They should be fine in detail and very small. The sub-dial should not be inset as it's on some replicas.

• Any quartz movement watch is probably a replica. Patek did make quartz models, but not of the 3919. You can detect a quartz movement by the "ticking" of the second hand. The hand will move only once per second.

• Many replicas are slightly thicker than the original.

• Patek makes this model in yellow, white and rose gold. Many replica examples are in rose gold. Look for gold hallmarks on the case back.

• Look for the Patek logo to be stamped (not engraved) on the buckle.

• Patek uses a faux ceramic style dial with the markers in raised relief. Many replicas use a printed dial. If you move the watch around in the light and look at the dial from an angle you should see the numerals slightly raised from the surface. Be aware that some higher quality counterfeits do emulate this look.

PATEK PHILIPPE

Calatrava Reference 3919

Picture courtesy of John Davis

Here is a genuine Patek case back. Notice the gold hallmarks. All genuine gold Pateks will have these markings somewhere on the case or case back.

This shot of a replica 3919 shows the weak spot: the position of the sub-dial at 6 o'clock. The sub-dial on this watch is too low on the dial.

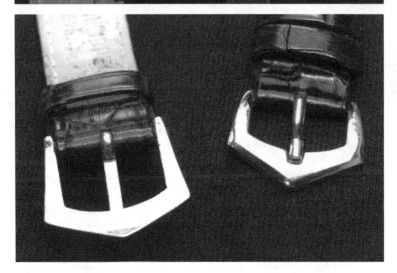

Here is a close-up of the replica's buckle and tang. While close in appearance to the original it lacks the gold hallmark stamps and the Patek logo.

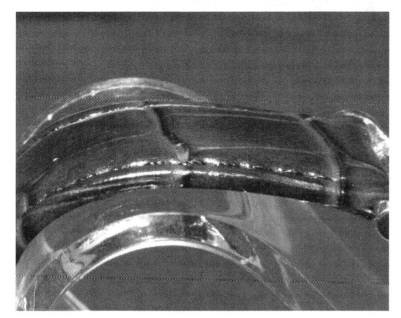

The imitation grain on this replica's strap is very close visually. Genuine Patek straps are made to exacting standards which are difficult to meet. While not exact, this counterfeit band is close enough to fool most people's casual examination.

This replica is a very near copy, until you look at the details. Notice the sub-dial position is too low. The case of the watch is also slightly too thick.

While this dial is quite good, genuine Patek dials have a very sharp, ceramic-like look to them. Pateks have the hour markers painted on the surface of the dial; you should see some depth to the numerals when you view the dial at an angle.

This genuine Patek 3919 shows a view of the dial and the blackened white gold hands.

Picture courtesy of John Davis

PATEK PHILIPPE

Nautilus

This watch comes in regular and Jumbo sizes.

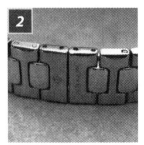 

[2] [3] This replica band does not have the proper clasp; it also has laser engraving on the outer side.

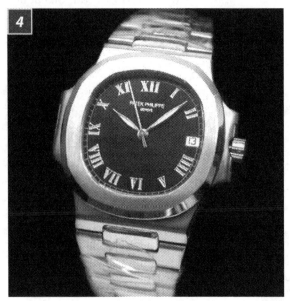

This is a replica of the Jumbo Nautilus.

Spotter's Tips

The fit and finish of the real Nautilus is much higher than any counterfeit. But as with many Pateks, the design is so simple that flaws aren't as dramatic as they would be on more complicated models.

The quickest flaw to detect is the date wheel font. No replica get this right on any Patek example seen to date. Dial quality is also substandard on many Nautilus clones. When possible, wind the watch; the crown should turn smoothly with a gentle resistance. If it winds roughly or loudly consider the possibility of the watch being a replica.

Also look carefully at the band. Many poor quality Nautilus replicas have a flimsy, light band with the links attached with pins (no screw heads). Also the clasp on the band is balky and inaccurate.

For the record, Patek does NOT use laser engraving on any of their models. Also, stay away from any quartz Nautilus (watch for a "ticking" second hand).

DANGER Most Dangerous

Some high-end ETA and Japanese models properly emulate the band and clasp. On these models the date wheel font is still incorrect. Patek uses a unique font that has not been emulated correctly to date.

Variants

There are several versions of this watch in different sizes. The replicas usually are of the base model, though the Jumbo model may have some recent copies. There are differences in hands (sword and baton) and dial styles; some dials will use stick markers while others will have Roman numerals.

The genuine Nautilus is available in stainless steel and yellow gold. Replicas are available mainly in stainless steel.

There are no genuine quartz version of this watch.

Nautilus Major Counterfeit Flaws

Genuine	Counterfeit	**Flaw Description**

Incorrect Case Back
The genuine Nautilus does not have an exhibition back. Note the visible plain movement in this example replica [6].

 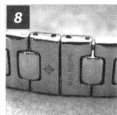

Clasp Design
The clasp on lower-end replicas is a visible flaw; it lacks the "fliplock" style and has laser engraving instead of the raised logo. Note that some replicas use pins in the band instead of screws.

Date Font
The date wheel font is unique to Patek. Many replicas use generic date wheels which make them easy to spot. This is common in Patek replicas. Some replicas even incorrectly use Rolex-style date wheels.

Comparison Photographs

Patek Philippe Nautilus

Replica >

Other Counterfeit Flaws

- There are two styles of hands on the Patek Nautilus. Replicas come with both styles.

- The genuine case back is solid, not exhibition.

- The "V" on the dial should be facing upright, not inverted. Some replicas get this wrong.

- The band should have screws instead of pins.

PATEK PHILIPPE

Rolex

 *Daytona (Current)*

 *Anniversary "Green" Submariner*

 *Daytona (80's)*

 *Day Date*

 *"Paul Newman" Daytona*

 *DateJust*

 *Submariner*

 *Yachtmaster*

 *"Red" Submariner*

 *Explorer*

 *"Double Red" Sea-Dweller*

 *GMT Master II*

 *Sea-Dweller*

 *Explorer II*

Rolex is probably copied more than any other watch brand in the world. The brand is always in high demand and brings in a great deal of cash from the secondary markets. This means there is a never-ending source of customers for Rolex products.

The counterfeiters capitalize on the fact that Rolex seldom changes their models, and on the large replacement parts market to produce some very good replicas of original Rolex models.

Rolex has countered the replica threat in the last couple of years with a few security features in their latest offerings. Rolex currently etches a very small (invisible to the naked eye) crown at the 6 o'clock position on the watch crystal.

Recent Rolex models seen at the 2004 show in Basel have shown watches with the name "Rolex" engraved on the dial sides under the crystal. Since neither is consistently used across the current product line it remains to be seen how effective these measures will be.

Even with these new anti-counterfeiting methods in place, there still is a huge market of pre-owned Rolex watches that are vulnerable to being confused with the higher-end replicas.

The models that seem to get copied the most are: Submariner, Day Date (President), DateJust, Sea-Dweller, Explorer II, GMT II, and Daytona.

Note that the trend currently in Rolex counterfeits is to produce replicas of "vintage" models. That means replica "Double Red" Sea-Dwellers and counterfeit 1980s-style Daytonas using Poljot movements. Always be suspicious of a 40-year old watch that looks brand new.

Rolex Replica Grades

Many replica sellers try to confuse the issue on the quality of their goods by referring to "A++" or "Category 1" watches. When it comes down to it they break down into simple categories:

Poor – No observant person would ever confuse these examples with the real watch. They are cheap and flimsy, made out of poor quality pot metal and in some cases plastic.

The band links are secured with pins instead of screws, and may even have see-through plastic case backs that show off the cheap Asian movement. These also sometimes use quartz movements which result in a "tick" in the movement of the second hand.

Average – The average Rolex replica would pass the "Sleeve" test (viewed on the wrist from a distance), but would fall flat on closer examination. They have incorrect bezel inserts and date wheel fonts. Watch for poor magnification from the cyclops on Submariners.

High-end – The better quality counterfeits still suffer from bad bezel inserts (particularly the bezel pearl, which is not inset), but the task of picking them out becomes much more difficult with the ability to fit genuine parts to these examples. More than one replica submariner is floating around with a genuine bezel. The easiest way to identify these watches is to look for the correct cyclops magnification and the right font on the date wheel. This will be examined in detail in this section for each model.

Achilles Heel: The Band

One of the weak points of all Rolex replicas is the metal band. The quality is usually poorer than a genuine model.

Most notable is the light weight and cheap feel of most replica bands. Also look for screws attaching the links instead of pins that some low quality counterfeits use. Note that Rolex did use rivets and folded links in some older (vintage) models.

Rolex Accessories

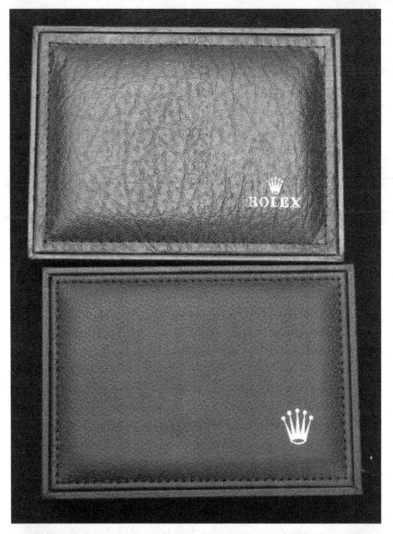

There are several versions of Rolex boxes that have been in production over the years. The example here (LOWER box) is from a 2003 DateJust. Notice the Rolex crown on the box. Some Rolex boxes use an embossed crown instead.

The replica box (UPPER box) is slightly larger and has the crown and logo. Also notice the difference in texture. The Rolex box is covered in leather, while the counterfeit box uses a vinyl surface.

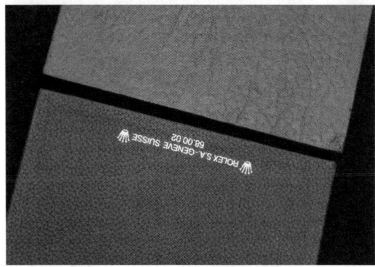

The bottom of the genuine Rolex box shows more gold stamping. The upper box, which is the counterfeit, does not have this detail.

Rolex Accessories

The top box is another replica. The printing on the box is rough compared to the genuine box at the bottom of the picture.

Rolex quality is consistently high. If there are flaws or irregularities in the printing or quality, it usually points to a replica.

The box on the left is a genuine Rolex outer box. Notice the bright gold embossed letters and the "OYSTER" text. The counterfeit box on the right has the Rolex logo printed with the surface as opposed to being embossed. It's really yellow instead of gold.

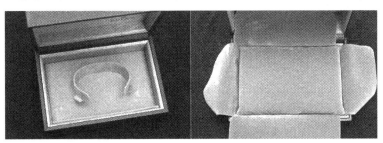

The Rolex box on the left has a built-in watch stand. The replica box on the right is still using the pillow-and-wrap interior that Rolex once used. The materials for this wrap are thin and cheap.

Genuine Rolex boxes of this style have the Rolex logo imprinted on the wrap.

Note: There are several variations on Rolex boxes over the years. As with all accessories they are a bonus, not a deal breaker. Even a real Rolex might be housed in a "replacement" replica box.

ROLEX

Rolex Serial Numbers

Rolex serial numbers are numbered consecutively as the model year progresses. Unfortunately Rolex takes liberty with their numbering schemes, which makes it difficult at times to determine the actual year a watch is manufactured. Below is a rough guide that will give you an idea of when a particular watch was made.

In order to find the serial number you must remove the band. It's engraved between the lugs at the 6 o'clock position. Some rare vintage Rolexes, like the COMEX Sea-Dweller, have the serial number engraved on the case back.

Serial Number	Year
F xxx,xxx	From February 2003
Y xxx,xxx	From April 2002
K xxx,xxx	From August 2001
P xxx,xxx	From April 2000
A xxx,xxx	1998 - 2000
U xxx,xxx	1997 - 1998
T xxx,xxx	1996 - 1998
W xxx,xxx	1995 - 1998
S xxx,xxx	1993
C xxx,xxx	1992
N xxx,xxx	1991
X xxx,xxx	1991
E xxx,xxx	From January 1990
L xxx,xxx	1989
R xxx,xxx	From August 1987
9 xxx,xxx	From July 1986

Rolex Movements versus ETA

This is a Rolex 3130 Movement, used in previous models of Day Dates. Notice the gilt engraving on the movement. Other trademarks of Rolex are the Red and gold gears, and the slotted rotor.

Here is an ETA 2836, used in a Rolex Submariner replica. It has a gold-tone finish, compared to the polished steel look of a genuine Rolex movement. It lacks the slotted rotor and red gears that a genuine Rolex movement uses.

Note the rotor states "25 jewels." A 3035 movement, which the genuine Rolex Submariner uses, has 31 jewels.

This is an ETA 2892-A2, used in a GMT Master II replica. The notable thing about this movement is that it emulates the GMT hand of a genuine Rolex correctly. Unlike earlier GMT Master II replicas that had a fourth hand that functioned like a 24 hour hand, this movement can actually perform like the genuine.

ROLEX

Case and Band Numbers

Case Numbers

Every Rolex model has a unique case number. This is the number that is embossed on the case back sticker. When purchasing a watch, if it has a sticker, make sure the number on that sticker matches the correct case number. This number is also on the inside of the case back.

This number is also located between the lugs at the 12 o'clock position.

Band Numbers

Band numbers are stamped on the inside of the band near the end link. This number indicates the replacement part if the band ever needs to be replaced. Each model has a particular band model associated with it. If for some reason the band number does not fit with the model, it may be an aftermarket band or a counterfeit watch.

Below is a small sample of the case numbers that are associated with each model:

Model Name	Stainless Steel	Two-Tone	Gold
Daytona	116520, 116523	N/A	116518, 116519
Daytona (80's)			
PN Daytona	6239, 6240 6241, 6263 6265, 6239 6240, 6241 6263, 6265 6240, 6240 6241, 6263 6265	N/A	
Submariner	16610, 16800 1680, 5513 5508, 6538 6536	16613, 16803	16618, 16808 1680
Sea-Dweller	16600, 16660 1665	N/A	N/A
DateJust	16200, 16220 16234, 16030 16014, 1601 1601, 6605	16203, 16233 16013, 1601 6605	16238, 16248 16018, 16078 1601, 1607 6605

Case and Band Numbers

Model Name	Stainless Steel	Two-Tone	Gold
Day Date	N/A	N/A	18238, 18239 18248, 18346 18038, 18039 18078, 18026 1803, 1807 1804, 6611 6511
Explorer I	14270, 1016 6610	N/A	N/A
Explorer II	16570, 16550 1655	N/A	N/A
GMT Master II	16710, 16760	16713	16718
Yachtmaster	16622, 168222	168623, 68623	16628, 168628
"Anniv." Submariner	16610LV	N/A	N/A
"Double Red" SD	1665	N/A	N/A
"Red" Submariner	1680	N/A	N/A

Case Number

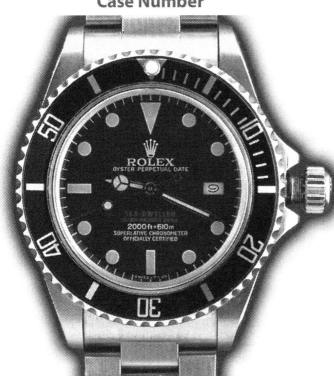

Serial Number

Serial/Case Numbers

Each modern Rolex has its serial number engraved on the case between the lugs at the 6 o'clock position.

The case, or model number, is engraved between the 12 o'clock lugs.

ROLEX

Rolex Accessories

The chronometer seal that comes with each Rolex is also duplicated. The genuine seal (left) is sharp and defined. The replica seal (right) is blobby with a thin gold coating on the letters.

The reverse side of the Rolex seal (left) has a hologram in the center. The fake seal uses a Rolex crown.

The genuine seal can be purchased off ebay for a few dollars. As with all accessories they should count as a 'plus,' but not factor heavily in your decision making process.

Inside the Rolex box (left) the logo and crown are silk-screened on the lower right corner. The replica box has the logo and crown printed on the center of the box. It's also printed smaller and not as sharp as the genuine.

Case Sticker

This replica has a non-holographic sticker on the back. Note the model number has worn off, but this is also common on genuine stickers after some use.

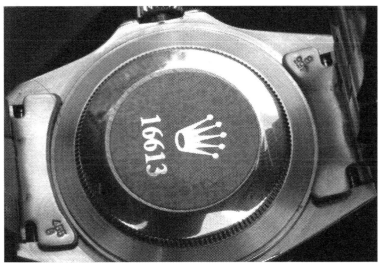

This lower-quality replica has an even poorer sticker, with no attempt at emulating the holograph.

Always compare the number on the sticker with the model of the watch.

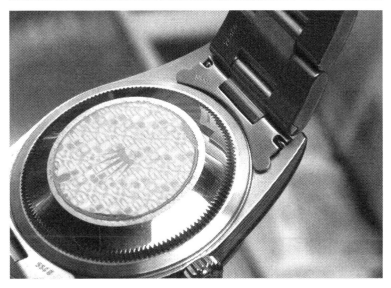

Here is a genuine DateJust case back with a holographic sticker. Note the model number has worn off.

ROLEX

Common Rolex Flaws

Construction Flaws
The date wheel on older models (pre-2000) should have "open" 6's and 9's. This means there should be a gap in the numeral. The exception to this rule is the Submariner and Sea-Dweller, which have used closed numerals for years.
The Rolex Oyster band has a smooth, solid feel to it. If the bracelet feels light or "tinny" when you move the links it may be an aftermarket band, and therefore potentially attached to a replica watch.
The stampings on the band tend to be poor on a replica. Look for well-defined Rolex crowns on the clasp.
Solid gold watches are heavier than stainless steel models. Gold plated watches weigh the same as their stainless steel counterparts. If the watch is supposed to be solid gold and it weight is light check other indicators to determine if it's counterfeit. This is where visiting a Rolex dealer and handling a genuine example can help you determine what the watch *should* weigh.
SOME (not all) newer genuine Rolexes have a tiny, almost imperceptible, crown engraved at the "6" position on the crystal. This crown is really only visible with a loupe. Some counterfeiters have taken emulating this to the extreme and have engraved a relatively huge crown on their crystals. This is easily visible with the naked eye and points towards the watch being counterfeit.
New model Rolex watches do not have holes in their cases for spring pins. This is because many of the models have moved to solid end links which do not require a spring bar tool to remove the band.
The only models that should use the Trip-lok crown (the crown will have three dots below the logo on it's end) are the Submariner, Sea-Dweller, and Daytona.
Rolex never made a watch with a display back.
Vintage Rolexes did not come with a holographic sticker on the case back. Rolex used a solid green sticker in earlier models.

Rolex Link
http://www.newturfers.com/
The new home of the self-titled "The Ultimate Rolex Forum (TURF)", this is a great resource for the Rolex fan. The forum can provide a great sounding board to help you in evaluating potential Rolex purchase.

Common Rolex Flaws

Construction Flaws

There are many variations to the Submariner. If you are interested in buying a rare vintage model be sure to consult an expert on the topic. If possible, ask the seller for any service records from Rolex that can help authenticate the watch.

When changing the date on a Rolex with a date window, the date should switch rapidly somewhere near midnight. If it changes slowly over time it's probably not a Rolex (or ETA) movement.

On Rolex date models, the cyclops should magnify the date wheel by 2.5x. In other words, the date should nearly fill the cyclops when viewed from directly in front. Many replicas don't magnify the date correctly; it will appear small and not completely fill the cyclops.

When adjusting the time on a modern Rolex, the second hand will stop moving as long as the crown is pulled out. This is called the "hacking" feature of the movement. This allows people to synchronize the time between several watches. Older Rolexes (1970's and earlier) and some lower quality replicas may not have this capability.

Rolex bands will have their links attached by either screws, or in some earlier versions, rivets. Rolex does not use pins to secure their bands.

When you adjust the date on a Rolex, if you wind the crown backwards (counter-clockwise) the date will click back one day at approximately 6 o'clock. Some ETA movements will also do this change.

Rolex models with Solid End Links (SELs) will have a number stamped on the end cap of the link. For example, on a Day-Date with SELs there will be a "55" or "55B" stamped on the end of the link.

While vintage models may have had green stickers on their case back, they didn't have holographic stickers. Older case back stickers tended to turn into a dark green blob over time.

ROLEX

End Link Differences

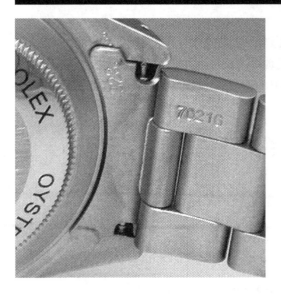

Hollow End Link

This is the style end link Rolex has used in the past. This particular design is used on older sports models. The end link is attached to the watch by a spring bar that fits through a loop in the link.

Solid End Link (SEL)

A number of Rolex models have switched to this solid end link design. These include watches like the Yachtmaster, Submariner, and GMT II Master. The solid end link fits within the lugs and does not overlap onto the underside of the case. Many replicas implement this end link poorly. They won't fill the space between the end links cleanly and won't fit flush to the top of the lugs.

▲ Real ——————→
◄——————→ Repl. ▼

End Link Comparison

Here is a view of a current production Submariner and a replica. The real Rolex has a SEL bracelet. This is notable by the solid link at the top of the band.

The replica has a hollow end link, which shows as a flexible link at the top.

Other Common Flaws

Genuine   Replica

Cyclops Magnification

A genuine Rolex cyclops (left) will magnify the date wheel by a factor of 2 and a half times its original size (2.5x).

Most replicas (right) either will have a cyclops that will only magnify by 1.5x or 2.0x. This is will mean the date will not fill the cyclops.

Crown Guard

The crown guard on many replica sports models is overly large. Notice on the genuine Rolex (left) the crown guard is small, and doesn't surround the actual crown.

On the replica (right) the crown guard is too large, and actually covers part of the lower half of the crown.

Crown Guard Example

Here's a high-end Explorer II replica. Notice how the crown guards nearly envelop the lower half of the crown. This is an easy and quick we to spot replicas.

Other flaws with this watch include the shortened GMT hand and the ill-fitting SEL links (notice how the end links don't line up with the top of the lugs.

ROLEX

Date Wheel Differences

Genuine

Replica

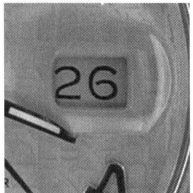 

 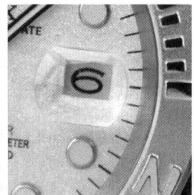

Wrong Style

The replica Sea-Dweller on the right is supposedly a "2004" model. Notice the open 6 on the date wheel, which is inaccurate for current Rolexes.

The genuine Sea-Dweller on the left shows the proper shape and font for the date wheel.

Wrong Font

These two DateJusts show the differences between the replica and genuine date wheels. Notice the replica numeral on the right barely has any serifs on the digit. It also has a nearly closed 9.

The genuine watch on the left has the correct yellow background color and serif digits.

Wrong Font

The replica on the right tries to emulate the current font used on Rolexes. Notice the difference in the shape of the "6." Also note the serif "tails" on the replica digit. The genuine watch on the right has a sans serif (not tails) numeral.

Wrong Wheel Color

Two-toned and solid gold Rolexes have a yellow background color to their font wheel. Not only is the replica on the right wrong in this regard, it also has an incorrect font.

This replica font style is common on lower-end Japanese and Asian counterfeits.

Clasp Hinge Detail

Replica Clasp Hinge

Many replica bands have a lower quality clasp. One of the things to look for on these clasps is an unfinished hinge. This is the part of the band that folds when you close the clasp.

On this replica you can see that the hinge is unfinished; it's simply folded metal around a pin.

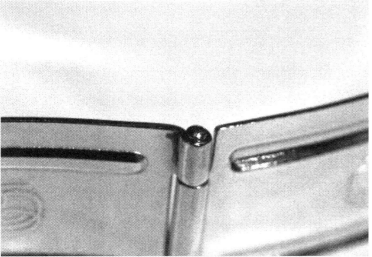

Genuine Rolex Clasp Hinge

Here is an example of a Rolex clasp hinge. Notice the tip of the pin has been rounded and the end of the hinge is finished. It fits together nicely and looks more refined than the replica hinge.

ROLEX

Daytona (Modern)

This example is based on the ETA Valjoux 7750 movement. Note the sub-dials are spaced too far apart to be accurate for the Daytona.

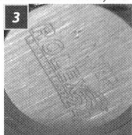

[2] A gold plated replica with day/date/24-hour sub-dials.
[3] Remember, only the Sea-Dweller has writing on the case back.

This example labels the sub-dials with their true function making it easy to spot as a counterfeit.

Spotter's Tips

Fortunately, there are no accurate replicas of the Daytona on the market today. All of them have some flaw that makes them easy to pick out. Look for the position of the sub-dials.

Always try the chronograph feature. Click the top pusher to start the stopwatch function and let it run as long as you can. If activating the pushers simply advances a sub-dial's hands by a tick it's almost certainly a replica.

Genuine pre-2000 Daytona's have the second hand at the 9 o'clock position. They use a modified version of the Zenith El Primero movement. Most high-end Daytona replicas incorrectly use a Valjoux or Valjoux copy movement that has improper spacing.

Post-2000 Rolex Daytona's have their 3 o'clock and 9 o'clock sub-dials slightly above the corresponding markers. Also, their second hand is located at the 6 o'clock sub-dial.

⚠ DANGER **Most Dangerous**

Currently, there are no accurate replica examples of the post-2000 Daytona. The replicas that have functional sub-dials typically use a Valjoux 7750 which has spacing that is too far apart.

Variants

Most common counterfeits are watches that have either non-functional sub-dials, or sub-dials that act as day/date/24-hours. These are easy to spot because the center second hand (which should be for the stop watch function) acts as the main second hand. Activating the pushers does not activate the stopwatch.

This watch is available in stainless steel, two-toned, and solid gold.

Daytona (Modern) Major Counterfeit Flaws

Genuine *Counterfeit* ## Flaw Description

Sub-dial Spacing
Replicas based on the Valjoux 7750 have incorrect sub-dial spacing. Modern Daytonas are based off of the Zenith El Primero and Rolex's new in-house movement, which have different sub-dial spacings.

Sub-dial placement
Post-2000 Daytonas have their sub-dial slightly offset above the centerline of the watch. This means the sub-dials ride higher than the 3 o'clock and 9 o'clock hour markers.

Wrong function for sub-dials
Many Daytona clones, whether labeled this way or not, have their sub-dials functioning as day, date, and 24-hour. This is most notable because the center second hand sweeps instead of the appropriate sub-dial (9 o'clock or 6 o'clock).

Comparison Photographs

Rolex Cosmograph Daytona
<Real Repl.>

Other Counterfeit Flaws

- Current Rolexes have the sweep second hand at the 6 o'clock sub-dial position. The center second hand is for the stop watch function.

- There are no genuine quartz Daytonas. If the second hand is "ticking" it's a counterfeit.

- Daytonas have plain case backs. Some replicas have "Rolex 24 hours" engraved on the back. This is incorrect.

- Attempt to use the stopwatch function. The center second should start to sweep and the bottom pusher should reset all sub-dials (with the exception of the second hand) to 12.

- On some counterfeits, the sub-dials actually function as Day, Date and 24-hours instead of as a chronograph. It pays to try out all the buttons and pushers on a watch.

- Many Daytona replicas will have incorrect crown guards (the bits of metal that project from the case around the crown and protect it from damage). These incorrect guards will be too large and surround the crown as in [1].

ROLEX

Daytona

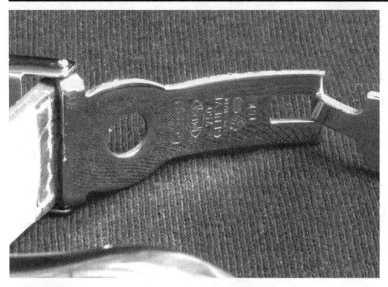

This is an example of a replica clasp. The details are poor, and it's even labeled with gold hallmarks and stamped 18K! It's clearly steel, and poor quality steel at that.

Here is detail of the other side of the clasp. The Rolex logo isn't sharp and defined.

Here is a close-up shot of a replica dial. Notice the poor quality of the letter printing. This is common with replica dials. Note the thick uneven letters and the blobby appearance of the Rolex logo.

This replica is dialed as a new-style Daytona (note the seconds sub-dial at 6 o'clock. The sub-dials are too close together, and on this model the upper two sub-dials are supposed to be slightly above the centerline of the watch.

Most of all, when you see this watch running you notice that the center second hand is the active hand, not the 6 o'clock sub-dial, which doesn't move. This is an easy flaw to spot.

The crown guard shoulders on this replica are too large; they almost cover the lower half of the crown. Rolex never made this kind of crown guard, making this another obvious flaw.

This replica is based on an ETA Valjoux movement. The spacing of the sub-dials is much wider than on a genuine Daytona. The second hand is located at the 9 o'clock sub-dial.

ROLEX

Daytona (1980's)

Genuine white sub-dial Daytonas of this vintage had black hands instead of the stainless hands on this replica.

[2] Poljot movement used in high-end Daytona replicas.
[3] Note the old-style clasp.

Note the poor printing of "Daytona" on this counterfeit dial. Dial quality is usually a good indicator.

Photo courtesy of Johannes Braunnarth-Knoebel

Spotter's Tips

Very similar in build to the "Paul Newman" Daytonas, the 80's models differ by having a black bezel and a different style of dial. With vintage models, be wary of watches that look "brand new." These watches are twenty years old and should probably show signs of gentle wear at the least.

Most replicas of this model use a "bi-compax" movement such as the Poljot 3133. These movements don't have a functional sub-dial at the 6 o'clock position (this is the "hour" sub-dial on the Daytona). On the replicas this hand is "fixed" at 12 o'clock, or follows (is synched) with the hour hand.

Replica sub-dials use plain stainless hands while the genuine model has either black- or white-tipped hands depending on the background.

Dial print quality is a good indicator on this model. Even the best-known replicas have indistinct printing compared to the high quality of the genuine.

⚠ DANGER **Most Dangerous**

The most dangerous model currently known is based on a Poljot 3133 or a Lemania manual-wind movement. It's fairly accurate but has a non-functional sub-dial at 6 o'clock and poor dial markings.

Variants

This watch has replicas in all the original colors: black, white, and silver dials. Bezel color is either black or stainless.

This model may be seen on a leather strap instead of a band.

Daytona (1980's) Side by Side Comparisons

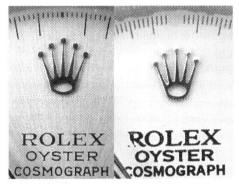

Left: Genuine

Right: Replica

Photos courtesy of Johannes Brauwnarth-Knoebel

Comparison Photographs

Other Counterfeit Flaws

- The replicas of this model come in three movement flavors: A Miyota movement, Lemania, and a Russian Poljot. They don't accurately reflect the sub-dials of the original. For example the Poljot is a "Bi-compax" which has a fixed (non-working) sub-dial at the 6 o'clock position.

  More recent Poljot and Lemania replicas come closer, but still don't have a working sub-dial at 6 o'clock. Try the pushers and make sure the sub-dials function as they should. These watches are thicker than genuine Daytonas because of the movement.

- These watches are from the 80's, and therefore should show some sign of patina or wear. If the watch looks brand new then the watch should be suspect.

- The crystal on this watch is Plexiglas. This means it's susceptible to scratches and gouges, unlike a modern sapphire crystal. The crystal might be buffed to remove scratches and will show up slightly wavy. If the crystal is flawless inquire about recent service.

- Dial printing is of variable quality on counterfeits. Use your loupe to examine the dial closely. While not to the same level of standards as modern dials, a genuine dial should still be sharp in detail.

- Test the pushers to make sure they work. Poor versions may have the sub-dials function as day/date/24-hour indicators instead of the stop watch function of the original.

ROLEX

Daytona "Paul Newman"

As with other Daytonas example the red "Daytona" script on the dial. Poor printing is a good indication of a replica.

[2] Note the incorrect "Oyster" on the dial.
[3] This replica's sub-dials are too close together.

This watch is marked with "Oyster" on the dial, yet does not have the screw-down pushers and crown of an Oyster model.

Spotter's Tips

The "Paul Newman" Daytona is a very famous and collectible model. There are accurate examples of this model in the replica world. Use this guide to spot these Poljot-based replicas. The 6 o'clock (24 hour) sub-dial is always frozen at 12.

If you're examining the watch in person, start the chronograph immediately and begin the rest of the examination. Observe if the 6 o'clock hand moves over the course of your inspection.

With any vintage watch that is 30 years old, it should show SOME sign of wear, even if it's been reconditioned. Older watches will show some patina.

🛑 DANGER Most Dangerous

There are rumors of examples based on the Valjoux 7750 movement. The best this author has seen are Poljot-based bi-compax (only two sub-dials work; the 6 o'clock hand is frozen) models.

Variants

Current variations include white dials with black sub-dials, black dials with white sub-dials, red dials with either white or black sub-dials.

Most replicas of this watch don't have proper functioning sub-dials. There may be some very rare Valjoux based examples, but for the most part they range from Poljot bi-compax to lowly quartz examples of horrible quality.

Daytona (Paul Newman) Major Counterfeit Flaws

| *Genuine* | *Counterfeit* | **Flaw Description** |

Dial Printing
Examine the quality of the "DAYTONA" printing on the dial above the 6 o'clock sub-dial. The letters should be sharp and have serif edges to each letter.

"Oyster"
Some replicas have a mislabeled dial which states "ROLEX Oyster Cosmograph"; this model lacks screw-down pushers, which is an indication of an "Oyster" case. Examples stating "Oyster" have either incorrect replacement dials or are replicas. [8] shows an example with screw-down pushers, but no "Oyster" on the dial.

Fixed 6 o'clock sub-dial
On genuine Daytonas of this model the 6 o'clock sub-dial is a 12-hour counter. On most replicas it's either fixed at 12 o'clock or moves in sync with the hour hand.

Comparison Photographs

Other Counterfeit Flaws

♦ These watches are from the 1970's, and therefore should show some sign of patina or wear. If the watch looks brand spanking new (no scratches, flawless crystal, no wear, etc.) then the watch should be suspect.

♦ The crystal on this watch is Plexiglas. This means it's susceptible to scratches and gouges, unlike a modern sapphire crystal. The crystal might be buffed to remove scratches and will show up slightly wavy. If the crystal is flawless, inquire about recent service.

♦ Test the pushers to make sure they work. Poor versions may have the sub-dials function as day/date/24-hour indicators instead of the stop watch function of the original.

♦ Models with black sub-dials should have white sub-dial hands. Examples with white sub-dials should have black hands.

♦ Most replicas of this watch are thicker than the original. This is because they use a different movement than the genuine Rolex.

Reference Link

http://samuelerinaldi.interfree.it/paulnewman.htm

An excellent resource for information and photos on the various models that are considered "Paul Newman" watches.

ROLEX

Submariner

The Submariner is one of the most recognizable watches in the world. It's also the most copied model in Rolex's line.

[2]: The cyclops magnification is too weak.

[3] This counterfeit Submariner has a totally wrong bezel insert.

Spotter's Tips

There are many variations in both genuine and counterfeit Submariners over the years. A true Submariner typically has a more substantial feel to it than the replica, and the build quality is always superior. Things like fingerprints on the dial or dirt under the crystal are clear signs that you may have a counterfeit on your hands; things like that would never make it past Rolex's QA department.

Look for bad bezel pearls and inaccurate cyclops magnification. Poor dial printing on replica Submariners is also easy to spot.

With the proliferation of Rolex parts on eBay (you can buy genuine cases, dials, bands and movements online) and other sites, it's possible to build your own "Rolex" totally from these OEM pieces. Such "Frankenwatches" can be difficult to spot since the process eliminates many of the flaws we've identified. When in doubt, buy from a reliable source or as always, from an authorized dealer.

DANGER Most Dangerous

ETA-based Submariners with genuine bezel inserts are potentially the most accurate replicas of this model. Usually the quality of the dial printing will be sub-standard on these replicas.

Variants

This watch is available in stainless steel, two-tone (yellow gold/stainless steel with blue, black, and serti dials), and solid yellow gold with blue or black dials.

Replicas vary the bezel insert's pearl quality greatly; some are close to the original, others are way off. Note also that the bezel insert can be replaced by the owner.

Some gold replicas use sold gold crowns, bezel, and center links on band.

This replica has a "purple" cast to the dial. Genuine two-tone dials are a vibrant blue, matching the bezel color.

Submariner Major Counterfeit Flaws

Genuine	*Counterfeit*	**Flaw Description**

Bezel Pearl
The bezel pearl is a quick indicator to examine. Genuine bezel pearls are inset to the bezel, with the metal surround barely above the surface. Most replicas have bezel pearl surround that sits on the bezel instead of being inset.

 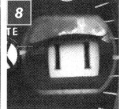

Date Magnification (Cyclops)
The cyclops on a genuine Submariner magnifies the date by a factor of 2.5. Because of the construction of most replicas the date magnification is usually at most 2 times. The difference is visible in how the date is framed in the cyclops.

Date Wheel Font
Current Rolexes should have a bolder more sans-serif font to them. The counterfeiters still have not replicated the new Rolex date font. Take a few minutes and visit a genuine Rolex dealer and examine the date wheel.

Comparison Photographs

Other Counterfeit Flaws

- The crown should be one piece, meaning the logo should not be glued to the end of the crown.

- When you unscrew the crown there should be a black rubber O-ring around the stem on current models.

- The date wheel font should have "closed" "6"s and "9"s. This means there should be no gap in the numeral.

- Current Submariners (2004+) don't have holes in the side of the case.

Alignment of Dial Printing
The "M" in 300m will line up with the "M" in Chronometer on a genuine Submariner (left).

Notice the poor dial printing on the replica (right).

ROLEX

"Red" Submariner

This example has the correct date wheel font but lacks the proper cyclops and bezel pearl.

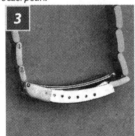

[2] Note the protruding crystal.
[3] Flip-lock clasp and screws in the band like the original.

These hour markers have no luminescence. They are painted yellow to imitate the patina associated with aging. Note the closed 6s in the "660ft" on the dial. They are open on the genuine watch.

Spotter's Tips

The genuine "Red" Submariner is a rare and collectible watch today. It's differentiated from a normal Submariner by the red text on the dial. Made some thirty years ago, they are becoming very valuable which of course spurs replica manufacturers to create copies.

The replicas of this watch all exhibit similar traits: they use an acrylic crystal like the genuine, they have poor date magnification, they use a cheap bezel pearl, and many try to "age" the markers of the watch by dyeing them yellowish.

The dial quality is typically poor in comparison to the genuine. Age and wear of genuine watches can make this a difficult test at times. Always look at the watch as a whole piece. Attention to detail will aid you in your examination.

DANGER Most Dangerous

Currently there are some convincing Miyota movement counterfeit red Subs on the market. They still are flawed; from the dial quality to the bezel pearl.

Variants

There are Japanese and ETA versions of this watch; both are very similar. Newer Japanese movement-based models have a more accurate bold-faced date font, but still lack adequate magnification from the cyclops.

By the way, there is no "hologram" sticker for this model. Be wary of any red Submariner that has a hologram sticker attached to the case back.

"Red" Submariner Major Counterfeit Flaws

Genuine	Counterfeit	Flaw Description

Date Magnification

The genuine Submariner has a 2.5x magnification of the date wheel through the cyclops. The date should nearly fill the width of the cyclops when viewed head-on. Most replicas have a 1.5x or 2x magnification which is visibly smaller than normal.

Hour Markers

Genuine examples of this watch originally had white luminous hour markers. These markers tend to yellow unevenly over time. This patina affects each watch differently. Replicas tend to make yellow markers that emulate this affect.

 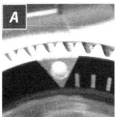

Bezel Pearl

As with most Rolex Submariners, the bezel pearl is a good indicator of authenticity. A genuine pearl will glow when viewed in the dark. Replicas tend to use a non-luminescent plastic dot in place of the true pearl.

Comparison Photographs

"Red" Submariner — Replica — Real

Other Counterfeit Flaws

♦ Dial printing should be strong and consistent.

♦ Vintage date wheels tend to have bolder fonts than current models. Remember, they didn't have laser printing back then. Use a loupe to look carefully at the date wheel.

♦ The crystal is plastic and protrudes from the case. Plastic (acrylic) crystals resist fingerprints better than sapphire crystals, yet they tend to scratch easier.

♦ Vintage Rolexes have slightly larger case holes for the spring-bars than current models. The shoulders of the case also are bigger than the current designs. Be wary of replicas of current Submariners with red-lettered dials, but no other difference.

♦ The crystal cyclops should magnify the date by 2.5x. Poorer quality counterfeits have horrible magnification.

Reference Link

www.redwatches.com

This is one of the best reference site for rare Rolex "red" models. Plenty of text and photographs simplifies research.

ROLEX

"Double-Red" Sea-Dweller

This example has an incorrect crown and a modern-style gas valve at 9 o'clock on the case side.

[2] Dial printing on this example is sharp. Note the aged markers.
[3] The serial and model numbers are engraved between the lugs.

The bezel pearl on this replica is poor. Note also the date wheel is not centered in the window.

Spotter's Tips

The "Double Red" Sea-Dwellers are rare watches. No one will have "several", nor should they appear new. These watches are 30 years old and should show some sign of patina, unless recently serviced by Rolex.

The crystal on this watch is acrylic and might show signs of scratching or gouging. This is normal and actually adds "character." Other signs of wear include an aging of the hour markers that tends to give them a yellowing cast. This patina is usually uneven with lighter edges. Note that the hour markers should not look "painted" yellow.

There should be a small gas release valve on the case side at 9 o'clock. This valve is smaller than the gas valve on modern Sea-Dwellers.

DANGER Most Dangerous

There are high-end ETA-based counterfeits that use cases that are accurate enough to accept Rolex OEM parts. The most obvious tip-off to these watches is the dial printing and the poor bezel pearl.

Variants

Japanese and ETA-based examples exist, with different qualities to the materials used. As usual, the dial printing is poorer than the genuine watch and varies greatly from watch to watch.

This watch has been seen with fake "riveted" bands as well as more modern oyster examples.

Variants of this watch also include "COMEX" clones that emulate a famous model that was made especially for the French company by Rolex. These are fairly rare and easy to spot since they have a unique serial number engraved in the center of the case back.

"Double-Red" Sea-Dweller Major Counterfeit Flaws

Genuine   *Counterfeit*   **Flaw Description**

Case back engraving
Note the difference in the type of engraving on the case back. The replica model [6] uses a modern CNC engraving technique that is much sharper than was available at the time of the original design [5].

 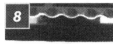

Gas release valve
The gas release valve should be smaller in comparison to modern Sea-Dwellers. Some replicas use a modern Sea-Dweller case to inaccurately represent the double red example.

 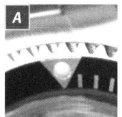

Bezel Pearl
The bezel pearl used in most replicas is simply a small plastic dot. It has no luminosity, and looks flat compared to the genuine watch. Some examples use the same insert that modern Sea-Dwellers and Submariners use, which has the bezel pearl sitting on top of the insert [1].

Genuine Example

Reference Link

www.redwatches.com

This is one of the best reference site for rare Rolex "red" models. Plenty of text and photographs simplifies research.

Other Counterfeit Flaws

- Hour markers on most replicas don't glow. But then again, a 30 year old watch may not glow as brightly either.

- Dial printing should be strong and consistent.

- Vintage date wheels tend to have bolder fonts than current models. Remember, they didn't have laser printing back then. Use a loupe to look carefully at the date wheel.

- The crystal is plastic and should protrude from the case and is slightly domed.

- The bezel pearl on replicas is usually terrible. Typically it's a small plastic ball instead of the inset pearl it should be. Remember bezel inserts can be replaced, so this should not be a sole indicator.

- Vintage Rolexes have slightly larger case holes for the spring-bars than current models. The shoulders of the case also are bigger than the current designs.

- The bezel turns clock-wise only. There are 120 clicks in a full revolution of the bezel.

- Examine the font of the bezel numerals. Vintage bezels had a thinner font than current models. Most replicas use a version of the current bezel, meaning the font may be incorrect.

ROLEX

Sea-Dweller

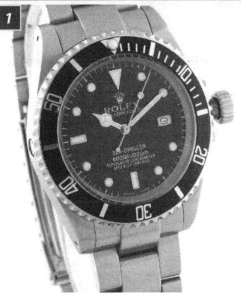

The Sea-Dweller is most notable for its' lack of cyclops. On this example the bezel pearl is definitely not genuine.

[2] This model has a rubber gasket on the crown stem.
[3] Note the over-large etching on the crystal.

Another example of a modern Sea-Dweller counterfeit.

Spotter's Tips

The Sea-Dweller replicas have many of the same flaws that the Submariner has. Read the profile on the Submariner; most of these flaws apply to the Sea-Dweller.

The case back on the Sea-Dweller differs from that of the Submariner in several key ways. First of all, it should have a 45 degree slant giving it a deeper stance. Also, there is engraved text on and around the case back on modern models.

At the 9 o'clock, on the case side, is a brushed steel gas relief valve. Counterfeit Sea-Dwellers tend to get this incorrect by making the valve too small or by not making it brushed steel against the polished case.

As with most Submariner variants, the bezel pearl is a good way to quickly determine potential authenticity. Recent updates from counterfeiters and the ability to replace the bezel insert with a genuine one means other indicators are necessary.

DANGER Most Dangerous

Newer, more accurate, bezel pearls on replicas make the ETA examples more accurate. Check the dial printing and the quality of the band.

Variants

Watches based on ETA, Japanese, and Asian movements are known, with correspondingly lower levels of quality (typically).

There are no genuine two-tone or solid gold versions of this watch. This is a tool watch, with no variations from the factory.

Sea-Dweller (Modern) Major Counterfeit Flaws

| *Genuine* | *Counterfeit* | **Flaw Description** |

Case Back
The Sea-Dweller is the only current sports model with writing on the case back. Also the case back has a 45 degree slope to the design, which is greater than a standard Submariner.

Gas Release Valve
Genuine Sea-Dwellers have a large brushed steel valve at the 9 o'clock position on the side of the case. Replicas have a variety of types of false valves, none of which have the matte appearance of the original. The replica valve is also only for show; it doesn't work.

Bezel Pearl
Most replica Rolex sport watches have an incorrect bezel pearl. It protrudes from it's metal surround instead of being inset. Note that this can be corrected by installing an authentic Rolex bezel insert.

Comparison Photographs

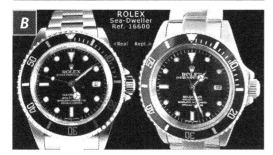

Other Counterfeit Flaws

- Dial printing is suspect on replicas. It ranges from decent to extremely poor. Use your loupe if possible to examine the printing up close. It should be sharp and defined.
- The crown should be one piece, meaning the logo should not be glued to the end of the crown.
- When you unscrew the crown there should be a black rubber O-ring around the stem on current models.
- The date wheel font should have "closed" "6"s and "9"s. This means there should be no gap in the numeral.
- Watch for mis-printing on the dial. Fuzzy printing is a good indicator of a replica.
- There should be a rubber O-ring on the crown stem.
- The bezel turns clock-wise only. There are 120 clicks in a full revolution of the bezel.

ROLEX

Sea-Dweller

Note the poor bezel pearl on this replica. It's a quick way of spotting a counterfeit.

Make sure you check closely the quality of the dial print on any watch you are examining. Rolex dials are sharp and defined with no blunt, fuzzy edges.

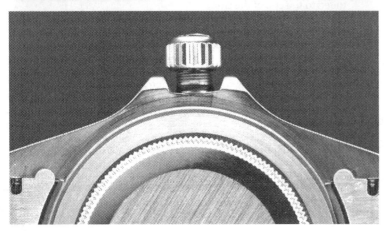

The replica here has an O-ring on the crown stem like a genuine Sea-Dweller, but if you look carefully you can tell it's missing the "groove" that the O-ring should sit in. This O-ring is simply placed over the crown stem.

This replica has an open "6" on the date wheel, which is incorrect for the current Sea-Dweller. The current model has a closed numeral font.

Note the circled crown etched on this replica's crystal. This crown is much larger than the etched crown on a genuine Rolex. If it's visible to the naked eye it's not genuine.

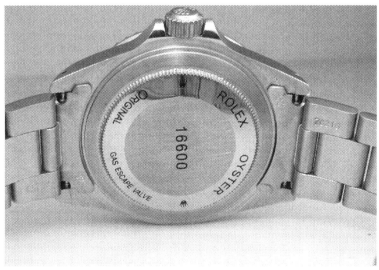

This Sea-Dweller replica has the model number incorrectly engraved on the case back.

ROLEX

"Anniversary" Submariner

This example has the correct Maxi-dial but lacks the proper "fat" minute hand. Note the bad bezel pearl.

[2] Weak dial printing is a good indicator of a replica.
[3] Genuine "Green" Submariners don't have spring-bar holes.

This example has a slightly better bezel pearl, but does not have the Maxi-dial hour markers or "fat" minute hand.

Spotter's Tips

In 2003 Rolex celebrated the 50th anniversary of the Submariner by releasing a special edition. This watch has several modifications from the base Submariner, such as a "Maxi" dial, "fat" minute hand, and most notably a green bezel insert instead of the standard black one.

Many replicas miss one of these modifications, most notably they don't get the hour markers correct on the dial (Maxi dial markers are 50% larger than a standard Submariner), or they miss the "fat" hour hand.

Since this is a modern Rolex it should have the current Rolex date wheel font, i.e. with no gap or serifs.

Always examine the bezel pearl. Most counterfeits use an aftermarket bezel that does not have the proper inset pearl.

The magnification of the cyclops on counterfeits is weak compared to the genuine watch (it should be 2.5x, while most replicas use 1.5x).

DANGER Most Dangerous

ETA-based examples with a proper (at least close) bezel pearl and correct dial are known to exist. While some even try to perfect the date wheel font, it's still not 100% accurate when compared to a genuine Rolex.

Variants

There are examples that have a green dial as well as a green bezel insert. Also, several fantasy dials labeled as "Frogmariner" (green dial), and "Colamariner" (red dial) are known to exist. Read your dials carefully!

Japanese and ETA movements are known to be used.

There is no genuine two-tone example of this watch. It's of limited production, so be wary of someone with an "inventory" of them.

"Anniversary" Submariner Major Counterfeit Flaws

Genuine	Counterfeit	## Flaw Description

Fat minute hand
The minute hand on this model is wider than on a standard Submariner. Any watch with a standard minute hand is probably a replica.

Bezel insert color
The bezel color for a genuine Anniversary Submariner is a striking green color. Counterfeiters have tried to match the color but have had varying level of success. The color should be a rich green.

Maxi hour markers
This model Submariner differs from the standard model in the size of the hour markers. They are much larger than the standard markers.

Comparison Photographs

< Real   Replica >

Other Counterfeit Flaws

- Currently a rare model. People typically won't have 10 of them for sale.

- The Anniversary model does not have holes in the side of the case for spring bars.

- Normal Submariner flaws apply.

- The bezel turns clock-wise only. There are 120 clicks in a full revolution of the bezel.

- The "Swiss Made" at the bottom of the dial should stretch over a total of five minute markers. On many clones it only extends over three markers.

ROLEX

Day-Date (President)

Dial print quality varies wildly in replicas. This particular example is very close to the genuine watch, except for the horrible dial print.

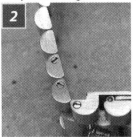 

[2] Look for screws in the band. This example is a President.
[3] Note the end link style. This is correct for a President band.

This example is easy to pick out as fake by the poor quality of the dial printing. The date wheel font bleeds into the background as well.

Spotter's Tips

Beware also inexpensive "bejeweled" versions of the Day-Date. Most likely they represent aftermarket diamonds (such as a replacement bezel or dial) or worse, a counterfeit that uses Cubic Zirconium or Moissanite stones instead.

This is a popular model to copy. Remember that this watch retails currently for $15,000 or more. It should "look" like it's a quality watch. Use your common sense as the first line of defense.

These watches are made of solid gold, so they weigh more than a stainless steel Rolex. They have a "heft" to them that is undeniable.

Look for gold hallmarks on the back of the lugs and on the clasp. These hallmarks are stamped instead of engraved.

DANGER Most Dangerous

ETA-based examples seem to be the most accurate. Still, the lack of weight for gold models and the typically poor dial printing are typically give-aways. Be wary for watches that have been redone with genuine Rolex dials.

Variants

There are many variations of this model, with a variety of dials, and with either an Oyster band or a Presidential one. Most examples are gold plated or "triple-wrapped". The gold plating may be thick enough to pass a test for gold content, but the watch in general is too light to be actually made of solid gold or platinum.

Any genuine dial style has been duplicated by the replica makers. Always handle this watch to get a feel for the weight; solid gold is heavy and platinum even heavier.

Day-Date (President) Major Counterfeit Flaws

Genuine　　*Counterfeit*　**Flaw Description**

Dial Printing
Dial printing is a good indicator of authenticity. Unless the watch has had it's dial replaced, a genuine Rolex dial has sharp printing without bubbles or pits. Always use your loupe to check the dial closely.

Weight
A big "tell" for watch is it's overall weight. A replica watch is usually gold plated and weights only as much as a stainless steel watch. True solid gold watches on the other hand are heavy and have a substantial feel to them. Rolex does not make this watch in stainless steel.

 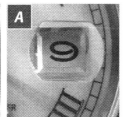

Date Wheel
The 6s and 9s on modern (post-2000) watches are closed numerals. Also look carefully at the date wheel. There should be no bleeding of the numbers into the background.

Comparison Photographs

Other Counterfeit Flaws

• Current Rolexes should have a sharp sans-serif font to them. The counterfeiters still have not replicated the new Rolex date font. Take a few minutes and visit a genuine Rolex dealer and examine the date wheel. Change the date a few times to see different samples.

• The day and date wheels on many replicas will not be centered properly in the window. This is a common problem.

• Genuine yellow gold Rolex Presidents have a rose gold clasp. This inner clasp is bonded to the rest of the band. It's a pinkish color and will stand out from the rest of the band.

• The crystal cyclops should magnify the date by 2.5x. Poorer quality counterfeits have horrible magnification. Be aware that genuine watches with non-Rolex replacement crystals may exhibit this problem.

• The day window at 12 o'clock should have its text centered in the window. If part of the day (or even the date) are cut off the watch may need adjustment, but is most likely a replica.

• Rolex has introduced the "Masterpiece" series in recent years [C]. All the flaws mentioned above apply to replicas of this model; quality varies greatly in the construction.

• On models with solid end links, when you are able to remove the band, look for a "55" or "55B" engraved at the base of the end link.

ROLEX

DateJust

Stainless steel Date Just replicas can be difficult to pick out. This example is fairly accurate. Look for gold hallmarks on the band.

[2] Fit and finish are poor in many replicas.
[3] DateJust replicas come in solid gold and two-tone as well.

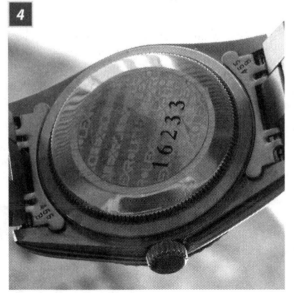

This is an example of the hologram used by replica makers. Note also the hollow end links.

Spotter's Tips

DateJusts typically come with a "Jubilee" band, which can be poorly made on replicas. Be aware that the band is usually the easiest thing to change on a Rolex.

DateJusts counterfeits are not as common as Day-Dates simply because of the latter's popularity. They are easy to copy by putting an ETA movement in an inexpensive real case. These cases can be purchased off eBay for around $100-$150.

Be sure to focus on the dial quality, date wheel, and cyclops magnification.

Solid gold models should have gold hallmarks on the back of the lugs.

DANGER Most Dangerous

ETA-based DateJusts seem to be the most accurate. Examine the date font and dial printing closely. These will be the most obvious flaws in this watch.

Variants

Replicas are known for about every variant of this watch. Oyster and Jubilee bands are the most common. As with most replicas the band is usually too light and feels "tinny"; i.e. it will rattle when flexed and generally feel hollow.

Rolex has made a number of variants over the years: two-tone, Tridor, Thunderbird; all have been copied by counterfeiters. Given the large OEM market for DateJust parts it's quite easy to reproduce just about every genuine variant on the market.

DateJust Major Counterfeit Flaws

Genuine	Counterfeit	Flaw Description

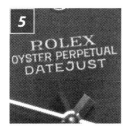 

Dial Printing
Dial printing is a good indicator of authenticity. Unless the watch has had it's dial replaced, a genuine Rolex dial has sharp printing without bubbles or pits. Always use your loupe to check the dial closely.

Hour Markers
Rolex dials are sharp and detailed. This means highly polished markers and defined luminescence on the hour markers and hands. Look carefully at the dial with a loupe; look for flaws or imperfections.

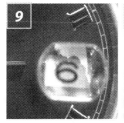 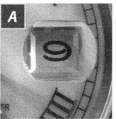

Date Font
If the watch is a post-2000 model, it should have a closed date font. Fonts with open 6s and 9s are for earlier watches.

Comparison Photographs

Other Counterfeit Flaws

- Gold models are heavier than stainless steel examples. Replica models are plated and weigh the same as stainless steel watches.

- Current Rolexes should have a bolder more sans-serif font to them. The counterfeiters still have not replicated the new Rolex date font. Take a few minutes and visit a genuine Rolex dealer and examine the date wheel. Change the date a few times to see different samples.

- The crystal cyclops should magnify the date by 2.5x. Poorer quality counterfeits have horrible magnification. Be aware that genuine watches with non-Rolex replacement crystals may exhibit this problem.

- The crown should be one piece, meaning the logo should not be glued to the end of the crown.

- Look closely at the date wheel font with your loupe (you do have one, right?). Poor quality replicas may exhibit ink bleeding of the font onto the date wheel background.

ROLEX

Yachtmaster

This Yachtmaster has the proper "fat" hand.

[2] An example of a solid end link.
[3] Note the lack of holes in the case and the slimmer look.

This replica lacks the proper cyclops magnification and the proper "fat" minute hand.

Spotter's Tips

The Yachtmaster is probably one of the easiest of the sport models to counterfeit since it does not have the "bezel pearl" that is the bane of Submariner and Sea-Dweller replicas. Nor does it have the GMT hand of the GMT Master II or the Explorer II.

To spot replicas of this watch, focus on the date wheel and the quality of the dial print. The printing should be sharp and defined, not bleeding or blobby. Also these watches are made of both 18k gold or platinum and stainless steel. They are HEAVY. The watch should have a substantial heft to it.

The genuine model has a "fat" minute hand; it's slightly thicker than the other Rolex sports model's hand. Many replicas don't use the proper minute hand making them easy to pick out. More modern replicas have successfully copied the hand.

Look for good-fitting solid end links. They should fill the space between the bottom side lugs and fit flush to the top side.

DANGER Most Dangerous

Stainless steel ETA-based models with the correct minute hand are the most difficult to spot quickly. Look to the cyclops, which tends to have insufficient magnification.

Variants

This watch comes in Ladies, Mid-size, and Full-size models. Two-tone models are only available in Mid-size, so if the example your looking at is two-tone Full-size it's most likely a replica.

Counterfeit dials are available in all the variants available for the Yachtmaster. The dial quality (materials and printing) tends to be vary greatly.

Yachtmaster Major Counterfeit Flaws

| *Genuine* | *Counterfeit* | **Flaw Description** |

Fat minute hand
The most obvious flaw on many Yachtmaster replica watches is that they are missing the "fat" minute hand of the original. If the minute hand is the same width as the hour hand the watch may be counterfeit.

Date Magnification
The date should be magnified 2 1/2 times (2.5x) by the cyclops when looking directly at the dial. This should fill the date in the cyclops. Many replicas have a magnification level on the cyclops of only 2x or 1.5x.

Second Hand
The red second hand should not have a visible red center hub. Many replicas have the second hand hub red. The second hand should also extend all the way to the minute markers at the edge of the dial. Many replicas have second hands that are too short.

Comparison Photographs

Rolex
Yacht-Master
<Real   Repl.>

Other Counterfeit Flaws

• Current Yachtmasters, as do all sports models, have solid end links (SEL). This means the ends of the band fit snuggly into the base of the case instead of having little "wings" the overlap the back.

• When you unscrew the crown there should be a black rubber O-ring around the stem on current models.

• The bezel on the Yachtmaster should turn both ways.

ROLEX

Explorer I

The simple design of the Explorer makes in an easy mark for counterfeiters.

[2] Note the obvious crown on crystal.
[3] Classic Explorer Is are popular and counterfeited.

Look closely at the dial printing on this model. Note the poor hour markers at 3, 6, and 9 o'clock.

Spotter's Tips

The Explorer I is a very simple and elegant watch. Unfortunately, the lack of complexity also means it's easy to copy. This also means there are less areas to check for "tells" about it's authenticity.

In examining this watch, we look for standard Rolex counterfeit flaws: dial and band. The dial printing should be sharp with serifs. Rolex does not release watches with blobby dial printing. Look carefully at the hour markers. They should be distinct and flawless. As always use light to charge the markers and check luminosity.

Also the band should be substantial in weight and feel "solid." Aftermarket and replica bands feel "tinny" in comparison to a genuine Rolex stainless band.

Without a date wheel or a bezel insert, the standard easy-to-spot details are unavailable on this watch. This means diligence on the other issues, but your best tool may be the saying: "don't buy the watch, buy the seller."

DANGER Most Dangerous

ETA-based examples with good dial printing are the most dangerous example of this watch as a replica. The simple lines means it's one of the easier Rolex models to emulate.

Variants

Replica dials are available in blue, black, and white. Note that Rolex does not make this watch available in two-tone or solid gold. The only color dial Rolex currently produces is black.

There are vintage versions of this watch without the metal hour markers. The dial has the same layout, but has applied luminescent markers at each hour. The dial on these watches is black.

Explorer I Major Counterfeit Flaws

Genuine	*Counterfeit*	**Flaw Description**

Dial Printing
Dial printing is a good indicator of authenticity. Unless the watch has had it's dial replaced a genuine Rolex watch has sharp printing without bubbles or pits. Always use your loupe to check the dial closely.

Hour Markers
Rolex dials are sharp and detailed. This means highly polished markers and defined luminescence on the hour markers and hands. Look carefully at the dial with a loupe. Look for flaws or imperfections. Some replicas don't have metal surrounds on the markers.

 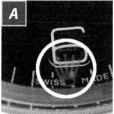

Engraved Crown on Crystal
Some of the newer replicas have a large engraved crown at the 6 o'clock position. New Rolex models have a very small engraved crown, so small it's invisible to the naked eye. If you see a crown on your crystal it's most likely a fake.

Comparison Photographs

Other Counterfeit Flaws

* The crystal of the watch should be sapphire. Counterfeit mineral glass crystals have a greenish tint to them.

Genuine Explorer. Note the clarity of the dial printing.

ROLEX

GMT Master II

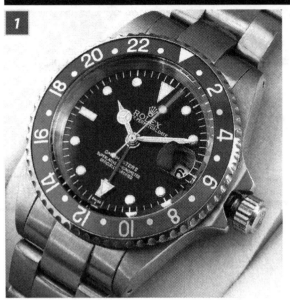

This counterfeit can be identified by it's short GMT hand.

[2] & [3] Replicas emulate all the factory bezel colors.

This is a poor example of a GMT II replica. Note the short GMT hand, poor date mag, horrible bezel insert, and sloppy crown guard shoulders. This watch is a good example of a poor replica.

Spotter's Tips

GMT Master II replicas were easy to spot until the recent addition of an accurate GMT hand; one could simply attempt to set the GMT independently. Now, with some very recent changes made by the counterfeiters, it's slightly more difficult.

Look for the dial printing and date wheel font. There are many poorly made Asian movement replicas out there that inaccurately replicate the bezel insert. Count the clicks as you turn the bezel. It should take 120 clicks to make a full revolution.

The GMT hand should extend all the way to the minute markers. Many replicas have GMT hands that are too short and too fat.

Watch for crown guards that are too big and envelope the crown.

DANGER Most Dangerous

New ETA movements with working GMT hand (not just 24- hour hands linked to the regular hour hand) are now being used in some high-end replicas.

Variants

This watch is available in both stainless steel and two-toned models. There are several variations in bezel colors including red/blue, brown/black, black, and black with gold lettering (two-tone).

GMT Master II Major Counterfeit Flaws

Genuine	Counterfeit

Flaw Description

Short GMT hand
The genuine GMT hand extends all the way to the minute markers around the dial. Replica hands are typically too short (and sometimes too wide).

NOTE: Some recent replica examples use a modified ETA movement that does correctly emulate this hand.

GMT hand not settable
Many counterfeits don't have an independently set GMT hand. It rotates synched with the hour hand, but is not settable separately.

NOTE: Newer high-end replicas may be equipped with movements that accurately emulate the GMT hand on the genuine watch.

Bezel insert color
The bezel insert colors are typically off for many replicas. The blue especially tends to be too dark or contain too much red. Examine a genuine model for comparison.

Comparison Photographs

Rolex GMT II

Replica >

Other Counterfeit Flaws

♦ Until recently no replicas have been able to emulate the true function of the GMT hand on the GMT Master. They would function as a "24 hour" hand, not settable independently from the hour hand. Recent copies of the ETA 2836-2 movement have introduced the ability for counterfeiters to provide the GMT functionality on their watches.

♦ The bezel should click 120 times in one revolution. The bezel moves in both directions unlike a Submariner.

♦ Many replicas have a GMT hand that is slightly too thick. The genuine hand is red and nearly as thin as the second hand.

♦ Dial printing is suspect on replicas. It ranges from decent to extremely poor. Use your loupe if possible to examine the printing up close. It should be sharp and defined.

♦ When you unscrew the crown there should be a black rubber O-ring around the stem on current models.

♦ The crystal cyclops should magnify the date by 2.5x. Poorer quality counterfeits have horrible magnification. Be aware that genuine watches with non-Rolex replacement crystals may exhibit this problem.

♦ The date wheel font on older models (pre-2000) should have "closed" "6"s and "9"s. This means there should be no gap in the numeral.

ROLEX

Explorer II

Notice the short GMT hand and the poor shoulders on the bezel guard.

[2] Is an example of a counterfeit modern Explorer II (Note the bezel and GMT hand), [3] is a replica vintage Explorer II.

The Explorer II has a shortened clasp, which this replica emulates properly.

Spotter's Tips

The Explorer II is very similar in function to the GMT Master II. They both have a 4th hand that acts as an hour hand to display another time zone. The major difference between the watches is that the Explorer II's bezel does not rotate.

Replicas of this watch vary greatly in quality, from poor tourist models with cheap Chinese movements and non-working GMT hands to top of the line ETA movements with the new 2892-A2 movement that has an actual working GMT hand.

The GMT hand should extend all the way to the minute markers. Many replicas have GMT hands that are too short and too fat.

DANGER Most Dangerous

New ETA movements with working GMT (not just 24-hour hands linked to the regular hour hand) hands are now being used in some high-end replicas.

Variants

Modern and vintage variants of this watch exist as replicas. This watch comes with black, white, and cream dials. The cream dial example is rare and very valuable.

Replicas of this watch have been seen in both white and black dial versions. The vintage Explorer II replicas have only been seen with the black dial, typically with aged markers and hands.

Explorer II Major Counterfeit Flaws

| *Genuine* | *Counterfeit* | **Flaw Description** |

GMT Hand cannot be Independently Set

Many counterfeits don't have an independently settable GMT hand. It rotates with the hour hand, but can't be set separately.

FLASH: Newer high-end replicas may be equipped with movements that accurately emulate the GMT hand on the genuine watch.

GMT Hour Markers

Replicas tend to have thinner hour markers on the bezel than genuine Explorer IIs. Notice the size difference in the triangles between the numerals on both bezels.

Short GMT Hand

The GMT hand on many replicas is too short: it does not extend all the way to the minute marker track on the dial. Replica GMT hands also are slightly thicker than genuine hands.

Comparison Photographs

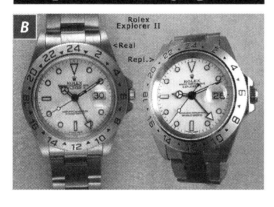

Other Counterfeit Flaws

- The magnification of the cyclops should be 2.5x; many replicas fall short of this. The date should nearly fill the cyclops.

- White Explorer IIs should have black surrounds around the hour markers. They should have black hands as well.

Genuine Explorer II. Note the black marker surrounds and GMT hand length..

ROLEX

Tag Heuer

www.tagheuer.com

Monaco

Tag Heuer is a popular brand that has several of it's product line copied as replicas. The Monaco and Kirium are probably two of the most successful in terms of accuracy. Careful inspection will almost always reveal the truth about one of these models.

For the rest of the product line the replicas tend to fall into the "poor" category: incorrect quartz movements or poor quality materials used in the case and crystal. Mineral glass is used quite often in these replicas. Viewed at an angle mineral glass tends to have a greenish tint.

Monaco

Sub-dials don't function properly on the replica. There is a marked difference in the quality of the materials used in it's construction.

Note the difference in the shape of the case and pushers.

Monza

Note the incorrect hands on the replica. The sub-dials also don't function properly. The center second hand acts as the main second hand, as opposed to the 6 o'clock sub-dial on the original.

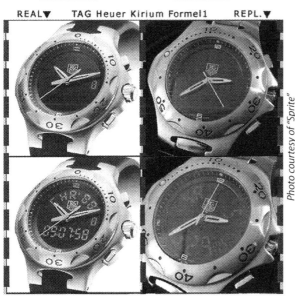

Kirium F1

While the replica is quartz-based with a liquid crystal display built into the dial it does not function like the original watch. Note the difference in the LCD display on both watches.

Photo courtesy of "Sprite"

Monaco

This color combination is called a "Steve McQueen" Monaco.

[2] Band quality is very important to review.
[3] This watch is also available with a black dial.

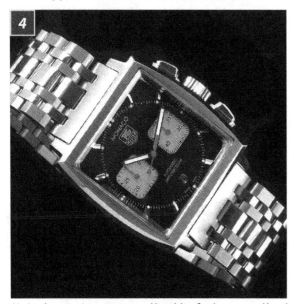

Notice the sweeping center second hand, but fixed true second hand at 3 o'clock. This is an indication of a replica with non-functional sub-dials.

Spotter's Tips

The Monaco has several copies produced, though most are of such poor quality that they are easy to spot. These low end replicas use poor quality materials that scratch easy and have a thick detectable "grain" which is usually the sign of low-quality steel. Genuine Monacos use high-grade stainless steel that holds a sharp edge and polish.

On a Monaco always start the stopwatch function with the pushers. To date there are no replicas that correctly emulate the sub-dials. Note that the center second hand is part of the chronograph function. The normal second hand is located at the 3 o'clock sub-dial.

The date window on many replicas is also too small. You'll notice the date seems crowded or only partially visible.

DANGER Most Dangerous

There are some decent Japanese examples on the market, but none emulate the sub-dials correctly. With the popularity of the Poljot 3133 movement in the replica community of late there may be a functional sub-dial replica in the near future.

Variants

The blue-faced version of this watch is known as the "Steve McQueen." There are black-dialed versions as well.

Monaco Major Counterfeit Flaws

Genuine   Counterfeit

Flaw Description

Small Date Window
The date window on replicas at 6 o'clock is too small for the date wheel. The replica's date window is also too high in comparison.

Non-functional sub-dials
When the opportunity presents itself, activate the stop watch function by pressing the upper pusher. The center second hand should begin to move. Normally the center second hand should not move.

Dial Printing
There are differences in the sub-dial and dial markings. The quality of the dial printing on the replica is irregular in comparison to the genuine watch.

Genuine Example

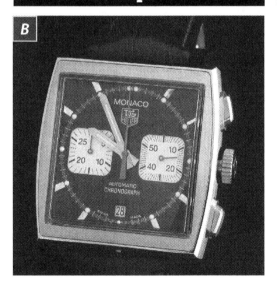

Other Counterfeit Flaws

* The quality of the case metal is an obvious flaw in many replicas. Genuine Monacos are highly finished, with deep-cut engraving and components that fit well together. Most replicas of this watch are made of much poorer material.

TAG HEUER

Vacheron Constantin

www.vacheron-constantin.com

Malte Grande Classique

Vacheron Constantin is a well respected brand name that has a lot of history to build on. Their latest offerings expand upon their reputation as respected makers of complicated watches.

Some of their recent models are beginning to see replicas produced of varying qualities. None to date have the same level of fit and finish of the original, yet some (such as the Malte Grande Classique) are close enough to pass a casual inspection.

With most Vacheron replicas the first detailed inspection will reveal them as counterfeit. They lack the finish to the case or the exact detail to the dial.

Many chronograph replicas have non-functional sub-dials, or they will incorrectly work as a calendar (day/date/24-hour). Activating the pushers will usually reveal these watches.

Display backs on Vacheron watches are also a quick way to determine authenticity. Replicas use the standard Miyota movements, or perhaps an ETA movement on some high-end examples. Vacheron highly decorates their movements, making copies easy to spot.

Malte Big Date

The genuine watch has a single date window with each digit of the date on a separate wheel. Most replicas emulate this as a single date wheel or with two separate date windows.

Note the difference in the dial and materials.

Royal Eagle Day Date

The quality of the materials of the replica are sub-standard in comparison to the genuine. Note the differences in the dial printing.

The replica watch has an exhibition back that displays an Asian movement.

Royal Eagle Chronograph

Note the differences in the sub-dials. The date wheels are substantially different between these watches. Note the sub-dial labeling on the replica indicating they function as day/date/24-hour.

Overseas Chronograph

Material quality on this replica is higher than average, but the sub-dials don't function as a chronograph. Note also the incorrect date window and active center second hand.

Malte Grande Classique

This replica has the proper sword hands of the original.

Spotter's Tips

The Malte Grande Classique is a simple yet elegant example of Vacheron Constantin's watchmaking expertise. Like many simple designs it's vulnerable to copies and counterfeiting.

When examining this watch, look for the correct wide sword-like hands. Some replicas use thin hands that look awkward on this model. Also look carefully at the sub-dial; the 15 and 45 should be angled inwards by 90 degrees.

The case back is a dead giveaway. The movement on a genuine Vacheron is highly decorated. Most replicas exhibit a inexpensive Japanese manual movement or a rotor indicating an Asian automatic movement.

[2] This replica buckle has the correct look, but is missing the gold hallmarks and logos. [3] Note the correct crown on this replica.

The lowered sub-dial is easy to spot on this replica, as is the shortened hour markers.

DANGER Most Dangerous

The manual wind replica with the proper sword hands is the most accurate of the bunch. It still is easy to pick out by the improper sub-dial. Also look carefully at the grain of the dial; most replica dials exhibit a poor quality pattern in comparison.

Variants

This watch has replicas in rose and yellow gold plate. It's also available in stainless steel which may attempt to pass as white gold.

Several examples with "diamond" bezels are known, some even with the properly oriented numbers on the sub-dial! Fortunately all examples are easily spotted as replica by examining the case back.

Malte Grande Classique Major Counterfeit Flaws

| *Genuine* | *Counterfeit* | **Flaw Description** |

Sub-dial Placement and Markings
The sub-dial on replicas is lower than on the genuine watch. This causes the 6 o'clock marker to be removed. Note also the incorrect orientation of the 15 and 45 on the sub-dial.

Case Back and Movement
Note the incorrect movement and surround on the replica. Some replicas use an automatic movement which is also incorrect. Note also the mislabeled case back and lack of finish.

Hands
Several replica examples have minute and hour hands that are too slender or lack the proper three-dimensional appearance.

Genuine Example

Other Counterfeit Flaws

- Some replicas use an unusually large crown that looks out of place on this model.

Photo courtesy of John Davis

VACHERON CONSTANTIN

Grande Classique

Photo courtesy of John Davis

This genuine Vacheron shows the areas where many replicas fall short of the original: the wide sword hands, normal-sized crown, correctly positioned sub-dial, and the hour marker at 6 o'clock.

Photo courtesy of John Davis

Notice the detail in the printing and dial surface on this close-up of a genuine Grande Classique. Some replicas don't have the printing centered on the raised name plate. Also, look for the accent mark in Geneve.

Photo courtesy of John Davis

The movement in this genuine Grande Classique is highly detailed and includes gilt engraving. While some replica movements may have gold lettering, it's usually applique (like a sticker) applied to the surface instead of engraving. These applique letters are basically stickers and may fall of over time.

Grande Classique

This rose gold replica is one of the higher-end Grande Classique replicas available. Note the proper sword hands. It still lacks the properly positioned sub-dial and the missing 6 o'clock marker.

This close-up of the replica dial shows more flaws. Note the difference in the dial pattern details. Also, notice the difference in size of the cross and the length of the hour markers.

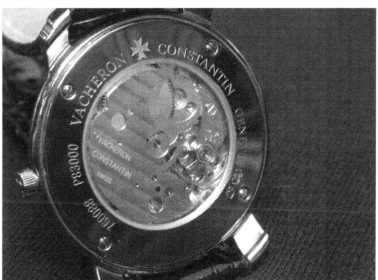

The movement in this replica is obviously counterfeit. Note the laser etching on the surface and the cheap stamped metal appearance. While the case back engraving is decent, it has the appearance of being plated over.

The display back window size is also smaller on the replica than on the original. Overall, this watch is easy to spot as a replica simply by examining the back.

VACHERON CONSTANTIN

Summary

Thank you for taking the time to read this book. I hope you've gained some insight into the variety and the level of quality that exists in the replica watch world. The watches profiled here are only a small subset of the counterfeit models available today. It's a dangerous world; take the time to gain the knowledge to protect yourself.

This book got it's start from me paging through the auctions on eBay over a period of a year. There were so many auctions that were blatantly fraudulent that it would make a knowledgeable person gun-shy about buying online. More disturbing was the more recent trend of subtle fraud being posted daily on auction sites, mainly high-end replicas being represented as real.

I hope this book has given you the tools to detect these scams, as well as taught you a bit about buying watches in general. If I can save one person from the heartbreak of having their watch confiscated (Rolex will hold your watch if you send it in for service and it turns out to be stolen or counterfeit) I'll be happy.

Stay tuned for future books that will focus on a particular brand in more detail. Rolex will probably be the first subject; they are the most copied brand in the watch world today.

Remember above all, Caveat Emptor: Buyer Beware!

— Richard Brown

ChronoSafe

ChronoSafe is a company that provides services related to the identification and categorization of counterfeit watches. These services are available in a variery of formats, both multimedia-based and in person. They include:

- Seminars on Evaluation and Identification.
- In-store training for sales staff and appraisers.
- Replica Watch Report: a quarterly review of the state of the replica industry.
- Web Forums and Special Interest groups to discuss replicas and their identification.
- Web- and DVD-based instruction on the detection and identification of counterfeit watches.
- A certification process to provide a training ciriculum on replica watches.
- Counterfeit awareness materials in the form of posters, calendars, and online videos.

We are always looking for new ways to provide services and solutions to our customers. Please contact us if you have a special needs; we can tailor a solution to your circumstances. Our goal is to spread the awareness of counterfeit watches to those who are most vulnerable: the high-end watch vendor and collector.

ChronoSafe Media

14761 Pearl Road #159

Strongsville, OH 44136-5026
(440) 268-9966

admin@chronosafe.com

http://www.chronosafe.com

Advertising Space Available

Would you like your company or service to be visible in the next volume of Replica Watch Report? Contact us for reasonable rates at *ads@replicawatchreport.com*.

Colophon

This book was developed using Adobe's Photoshop and InDesign CS products. Microsoft Word was used to type in some of the text in order to provide spell checking and to hold ideas and fragments of text. Adobe Acrobat provided the tools to hone the book as a PDF and provide a direct link to the publisher. The acceptance of PDFs in the printing industry makes the Adobe tools invaluable to the author or small publisher.

I'm a believer in simplicity when it comes to fonts. This book uses Myriad Pro and Minion Pro for the body, and Rockwell Condensed for the headlines. All three are excellent fonts that hopefully provide a clear and easy text to read.

Why print in 8 1/2 x 11 inches?

My original plan was to print this book as a 6 x 9 inch edition with a wire spine. This would be easier to transport to flea markets, and the wire spine would allow you to fold the book flat, or open to a particular page. When I decided to make the color edition I was told I was charged per page the same cost no matter what the actual print size. In reality the 6 x 9 book was actually printed as 8 1/2" x 11" and trimmed down! Given that by going to 8 1/2" x 11" I was getting printing real estate for free I changed to the larger format.

This has actually turned out as a blessing. It's allowed me to offer larger pictures than I could have with the smaller edition. It's also helped me cut down on my page count, which directly affects the final cost of the book.

CPSIA information can be obtained
at www.ICGtesting.com
Printed in the USA
BVHW010153170920
588713BV00009BA/368